AMERICAN CORPORATE IDENTITY 2001

Editor
DAVID E. CARTER

Art Direction
Suzanna M.W. Stephens

Book Design
Rebecca Renzi

Cover Design
Graham Allen

AMERICAN CORPORATE IDENTITY 2001

First published in 2000 by HBI,
an imprint of HarperCollins Publishers
10 East 53rd Street
New York, NY 10022-5299

ISBN: 0688-17985-1

Distributed in the U.S. and Canada by
Watson-Guptill Publications
770 Broadway
New York, NY 10003-9595
Tel: (800) 451-1741
            (732) 363-4511 in NJ, AK, HI
Fax: (732) 363-0338

Distributed throughout the rest of the world by
HarperCollins International
10 East 53rd Street
New York, NY 10022-5299
Fax: (212) 207-7654

Printed in Hong Kong by Everbest Printing Company through Four Colour
Imports, Louisville, Kentucky.

TABLE OF CONTENTS

COMPLETE CORPORATE ID PROGRAMS

Client
  Traverse City
Design Firm
  Landor Associates
Designers
  Martine Channon, Soo Jih Yum

TRAVERSE
CITY

A World Apart

Client
Chris Collins

Design Firm
Clockwork Apple Inc.

Designer
Christo Holloway

Chris Collins Studio
35 West 20th Street, NYC 10011
(212)633.1670 Fax:(212)727.1518

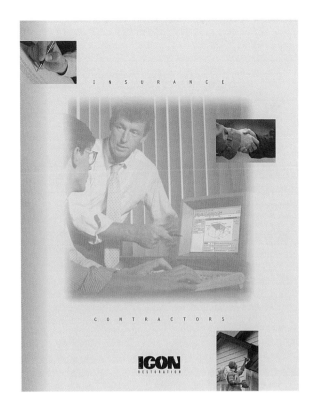

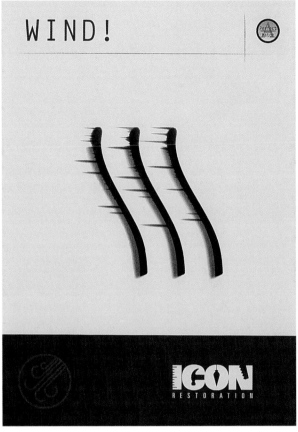

WIND!

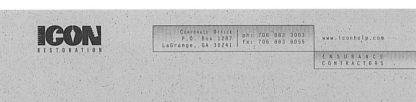

Client
Icon Restoration

Design Firm
B-Man Design

Designers
David Belmonte, Barry Brager, Eric Etheridge

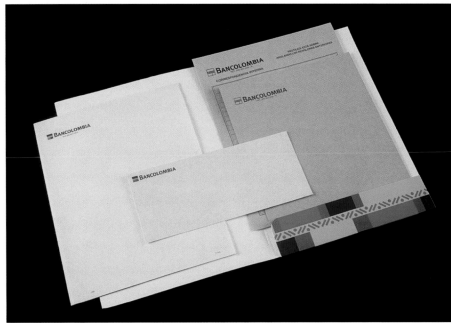

Client
Bancolombia

Design Firm
Interbrand

Designers
Interbrand Design Team

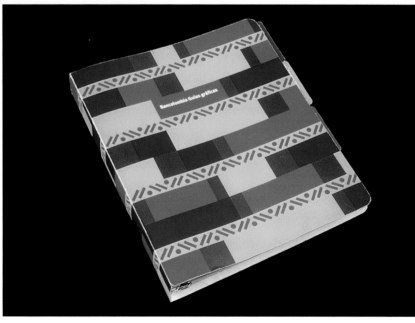

Client
  Nationwide
Design Firm
  Interbrand
Designers
  Interbrand Design Team

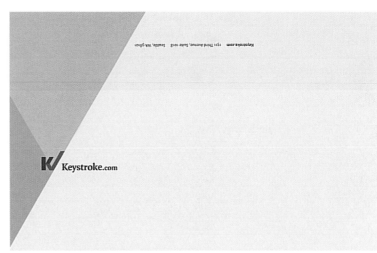

Client
Keystroke.com

Design Firm
Werkhaus Creative Communications

Designers
Thad Boss, John Burgess, Jodi Morrison

Stephanie Milrad
ASSOCIATE
CONSUMER LENDING

Keystroke.com
1511 Third Avenue, Suite 520
Seattle, WA 98101

T 800.664.1003
   206.625.1001
F 206.625.1011

stephanie@keystroke.com
www.keystroke.com

Client
    Bancomer

Design Firm
    Interbrand

Designers
    Interbrand Design Team

Client
Sirius Satellite Radio

Design Firm
Interbrand

Designers
Interbrand Design Team

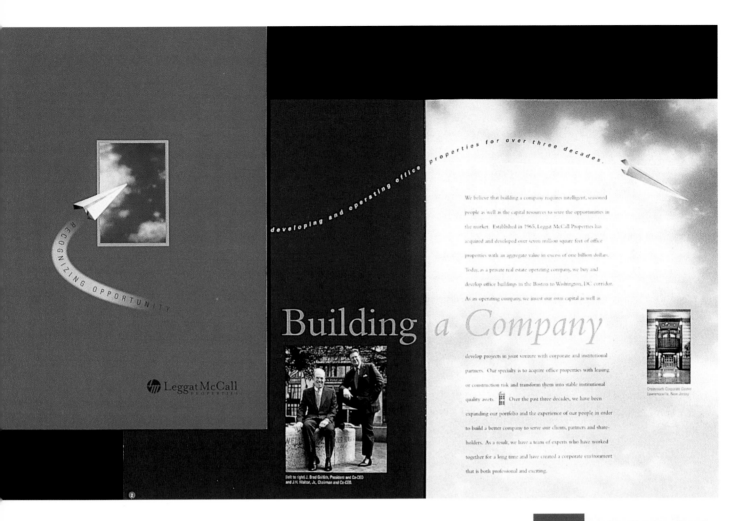

Building *a Company*

developing and operating office properties for over three decades.

We believe that building a company requires intelligent, seasoned people as well as the capital resources to seize the opportunities in the market. Established in 1965, Leggat McCall Properties has acquired and developed over seven million square feet of office properties with an aggregate value in excess of one billion dollars. Today, as a private real estate operating company, we buy and develop office buildings in the Boston to Washington, DC corridor. As an operating company, we invest our own capital as well as develop projects in joint venture with corporate and institutional partners. Our specialty is to acquire office properties with leasing or construction risk and transform them into stable institutional quality assets. Over the past three decades, we have been expanding our portfolio and the experience of our people in order to build a better company to serve our clients, partners and shareholders. As a result, we have a team of experts who have worked together for a long time and have created a corporate environment that is both professional and exciting.

(left to right) J. Brad Griffith, President and Co-CEO and J.H. Walton, Jr., Chairman and Co-CEO.

Crossroads Corporate Center Lawrenceville, New Jersey

Client
Legatt McCall Properties

Design Firm
Doerr Associates, Inc.

Designers
Linda Blacksmith, Lauren Jeuick

Eric K. Bacon
Senior Vice President, Director of
Corporate Services Group

Leggat McCall Properties LLC
10 Post Office Square
Boston, MA 02109
617-422-7019   *fax* 617-422-7002
mobile: 617-306-9210
eric.bacon@lmp.com

Profile

Leggat McCall Properties is a Boston-based, private real estate operating company. We buy and develop office buildings in the Boston to Washington, DC corridor.

Established in 1965, we have been in business for over three decades. During this time, we have acquired or developed more than 7 million square feet of real estate for our own account with an aggregate value of more than $1 billion. We have also managed over 15 million square feet of properties on a third-party basis for our partners and institutional clients.

We have over 100 employees and five regional offices. Our activities include acquisition, development and operation of office properties including asset and property management, leasing and construction management. We also provide independent project management services.

Client
  Dean & Deluca
Design Firm
  Landor Associates
Designer
  Jeremy Dawkins

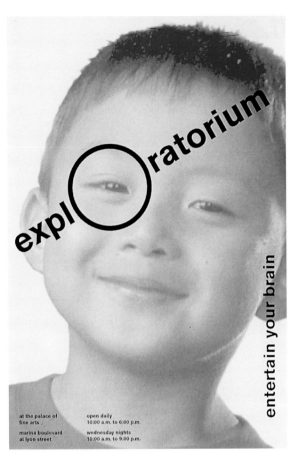

entertain your brain

at the palace of
fine arts /

marina boulevard
at lyon street

open daily
10:00 a.m. to 6:00 p.m.

wednesday nights
10:00 a.m. to 9:00 p.m.

Client
  Exploratorium
Design Firm
  Landor Associates
Designers
  Margaret Youngblood, Doug Sellers

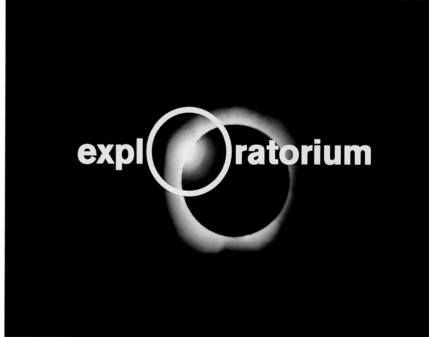

Client
Pathé

Design Firm
Landor Associates

Designers
Margaret Youngblood, Eric Scott,
Doug Sellers, Kirsten Tarnowski, Michele Berry

Client
Lois Allen
School of the Dance

Design Firm
Callery & Company

Designer
Kelley Callery

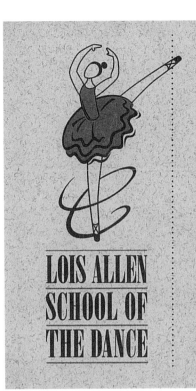

LORALYN GAUGHRAN
Director

Clarkton Shopping Center

PO Box 5842 • Clark NJ 07066

732-388-8288

A Complete Dance Program for All Ages
Beginners thru Advanced

LOIS ALLEN SCHOOL OF THE DANCE

Clarkton Shopping Center
Raritan Road, Clark NJ 07066
732-388-8288

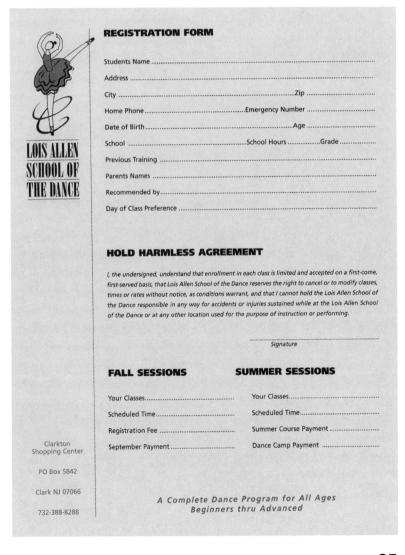

REGISTRATION FORM

Students Name ....
Address ....
City .... Zip ....
Home Phone........................ Emergency Number ....
Date of Birth.. Age ....
School .... School Hours .... Grade ....
Previous Training ....
Parents Names ....
Recommended by..
Day of Class Preference ....

HOLD HARMLESS AGREEMENT

I, the undersigned, understand that enrollment in each class is limited and accepted on a first-come, first-served basis, that Lois Allen School of the Dance reserves the right to cancel or to modify classes, times or rates without notice, as conditions warrant, and that I cannot hold the Lois Allen School of the Dance responsible in any way for accidents or injuries sustained while at the Lois Allen School of the Dance or at any other location used for the purpose of instruction or performing.

....
Signature

FALL SESSIONS   SUMMER SESSIONS

Your Classes...................   Your Classes...................
Scheduled Time..............   Scheduled Time..............
Registration Fee ....   Summer Course Payment ......
September Payment ....   Dance Camp Payment ....

Clarkton
Shopping Center

PO Box 5842

Clark NJ 07066

732-388-8288

A Complete Dance Program for All Ages
Beginners thru Advanced

25

Client
Brown Shoe Company

Design Firm
Kiku Obata & Company

Designers
Scott Gericke,
Amy Knopf,
Joe Floresca,
Jennifer Baldwin,
Carole Jerome

B

BROWN SHOE

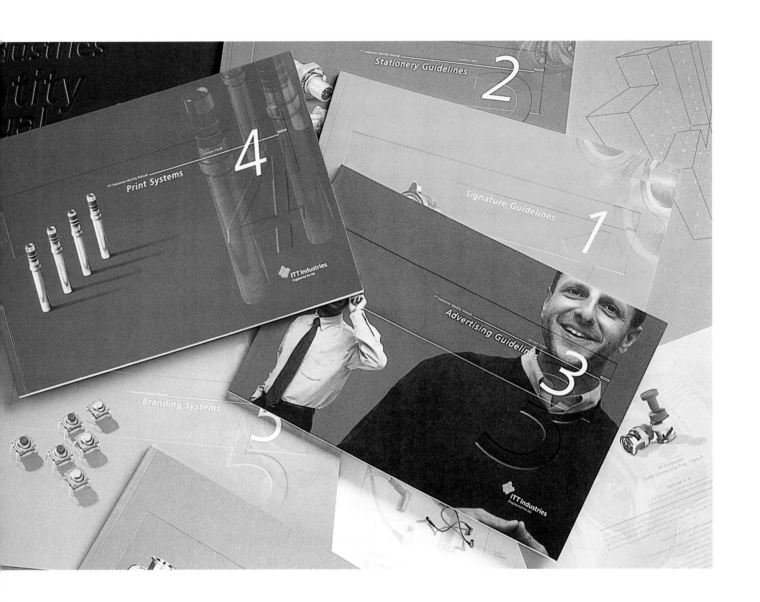

Client
ITT Industries

Design Firm
Landor Associates

Designer
Jamie Calderon

Client
    The Cleveland Indians
Design Firm
    Herip Associates
Designers
    Walter Herip, John Menter

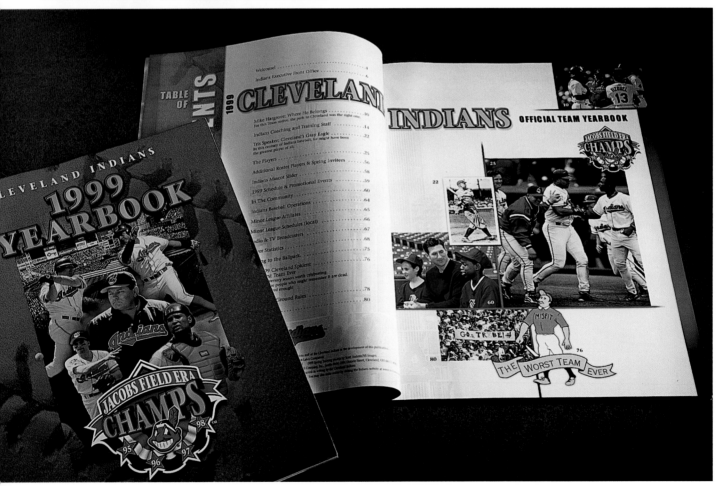

Client
Reliant Energy

Design Firm
**Lister Butler
Consulting**

Senior Designer
William Davis

Client
Solange de France.com, L.L.C.
Design Firm
Maffini & Bearce
Designer
Philippe Maffini

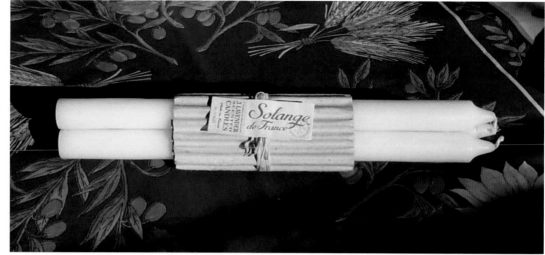

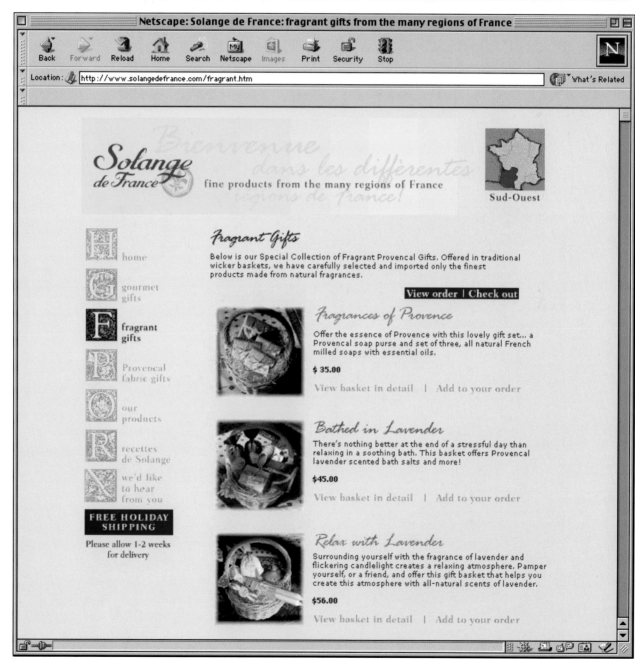

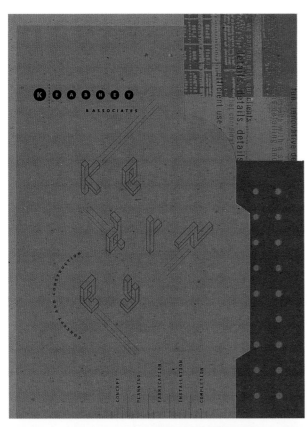

Client
Kearney & Associates
Design Firm
Gibson Creative
Designer
Juliette Brown

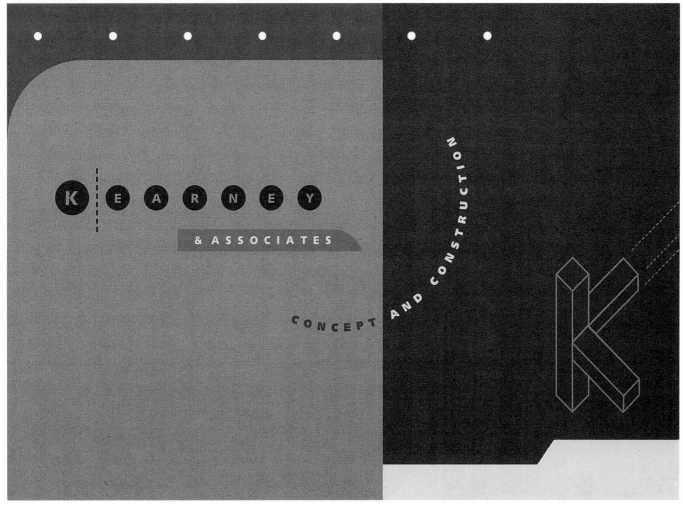

Client
Horizon
Blue Cross
Blue Shield
of New Jersey

Design Firm
**Lister Butler
Consulting**

Senior Designer
William Davis

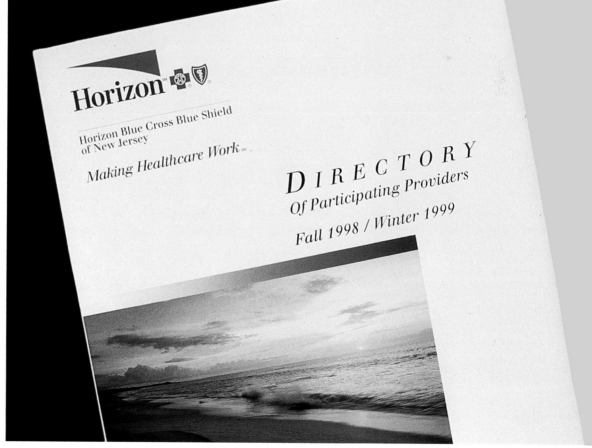

STONITSCH
CONSTRUCTION

Client
  Stonitsch Construction

Design Firm
  Bullet Communications, Inc.

Designer
  Tim Scott

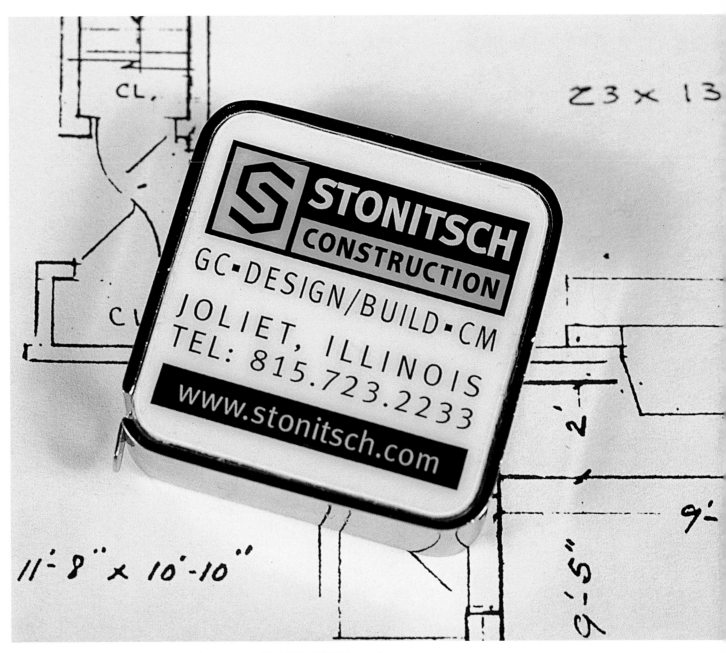

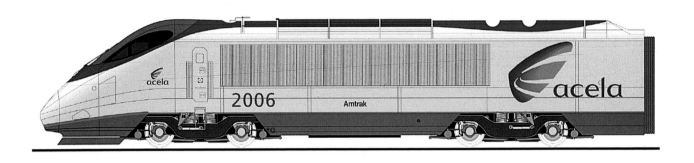

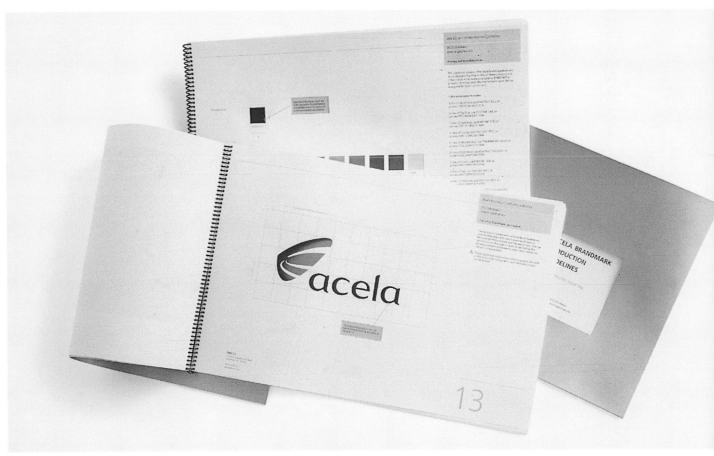

Client
Amtrak

Design Firm
OH&CO in collaboration with IDEO

Creative Director
Brent Oppenheimer

Strategy Director
Robin Haueter

Design Director
Mary Ellen Buttner

Designers
Michael Thibodeau, David Shields, Sally Hwang

Copywriter
Ginger Strand

Client
  SGI

Design Firm
  Landor Associates

Designers
  Patrick Cox, Frank Mueller

sgi™

Client
  Jwana Juice
Design Firm
  Cathey Associates, Inc.
Designer
  Isabel Campos

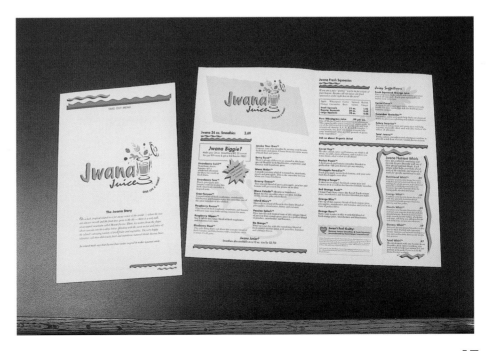

EarthLink™

Client
EarthLink

Design Firm
FOCUS Design and Marketing Solutions

Designer
Aram Youssefian

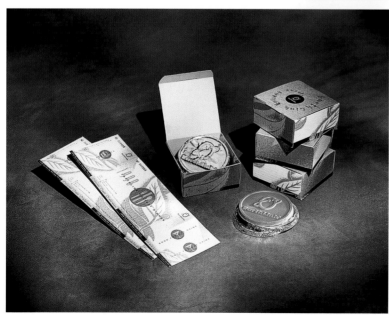

EQUITABLE
RESOURCES

Client
Equitable Resources

Design Firm
Kendra Power Design & Communication

50

Client
Tenaya Creek
Restaurant & Brewery
Design Firm
Creative Dynamic
Creative Directors
Victor Rodriguez,
Eddie Roberts
Designers
Dawn Teagarden,
Casey Corcoran

PACKAGE DESIGNS

Client
    1881
Design Firm
    Arias Associates
Designers
    Mauricio Arias, Steve Mortensen

Client
    Friendly's Ice Cream Corporation
Design Firm
    Luis R. Lee & Associates
Designers
    Luis R. Lee, Heather Van Loan

Client
    VDK Frozen Foods
Design Firm
    Interbrand Gerstman + Meyers
Designers
    Rafael Feliciano, Jillian Mazzacano

Client
    Bartolomeh
Design Firm
    Cullinane Design
Designer
    Emily Mann

Client
  Casa Cuervo

Design Firm
  Klim Design, Inc.

Designer
  Matt Klim

Client
  Pamela's Product

Design Firm
  Dickson Design

Designer
  Deborah Shea

Client
  The Quaker Oats Company

Design Firm
  Desgrippes Gobé

Creative Director   Design Director
  Peter Levine   Tom Davidson

Client
  Sherwin Williams

Design Firm
  Interbrand Gerstman + Meyers

Designer
  Mitch Gottlieb

Client
    Porex Bio Products Group
Design Firm
    Reed Sendecke, Inc.
Designers
    Design Staff of Reed Sendecke, Inc.

Client
    Unisunstar B.V., Inc. (VO5)
Design Firm
    Desgrippes Gobé
Creative Director
    Phyllis Aragaki
Senior Designer
    Deirdre Tighe

Client
    Watson-Guptill Publications
Design Firm
    Farenga Design Group
Designer
    Anthony Farenga

Client
    Casa Cuervo, S.A. de C.V.
Design Firm
    Klim Design, Inc.
Designer
    Matt Klim

Client
  Target Packaging

Design Firm
  Yamamoto Moss, Minneapolis, MN

Creative Director
  Kasey Hatzung

Art Director
  Lisa Hagman

Client
  Panache

Design Firm
  Walsh & Associates, inc.

Designers
  Miriam Lisco, Lyn Blanchard

Client
  The Limited Inc.
  (Victoria's Secret Beauty Co.)

Design Firm
  Desgrippes Gobé

Design Director
  Lori Yi Golden

Senior Designers
  Marie-Laure Bonnet, Peggy Wong

Client
  Eastman Kodak Company

Design Firm
  Icon Graphics, Inc.

Designers
  Icon Graphics, Inc.

Client
  Teisseire

Design Firm
  Desgrippes Gobé

Designers
  Desgrippes Gobé

Client
  Pollenex/The Holmes Group

Design Firm
  Arc Design

Designers
  Jac Phillips, Kevin O'Leary, Kevin Bergen, Todd Kinniburgh

Client
  Brown Shoe Company

Design Firm
  Kiku Obata & Company

Designer
  Scott Gericke

Illustrator   Copywriter
  Al Sacui   Carole Jerome

Client
  Amanda Hunt-Taylor

Design Firm
  Taylor Designs

Designer
  Jennifer Whitaker

60

Client
Canandaigua Wine Co.

Design Firm
McElveney & Palozzi Design Group, Inc.

Designers
Steve Palozzi, William McElveney

Client
Robinson Knife Company

Design Firm
Michael Orr + Associates, Inc.

Designers
Michael R. Orr, Thomas Freeland

Client
Target Stores

Design Firm
Design Guys

Art Director
Steven Sikora

Designer
Dawn Selg

Client
General Motors

Design Firm
Interbrand Gerstman + Meyers

Designers
Juan Concepcion, Annie Baker

61

Client
Kellogg Company

Design Firm
Interbrand Gerstman + Meyers

Designers
Jeff Zack and Staff

Client
Nestlé USA—Chocolate & Confections

Design Firm
Thompson Design Group

Designers
Felicia Utomo, Elizabeth Berta

Client
Barnes and Watson

Design Firm
Walsh & Associates, inc.

Designers
Lyn Blanchard, Miriam Lisco

Client
Delicious Brands, Inc.

Design Firm
Harbauer Bruce Nelson Design

Designer
Steve Walker

Client
  Bestfoods
Design Firm
  R. Bird & Company
Designer
  Joe Favata

Client
  Hewlett Packard
Design Firm
  Laura Coe Design Assoc
Designer
  Denise Heisey

Client
  Borden Foods Corporation
Design Firm
  Harbauer Bruce Nelson Design
Designer
  Steve Walker

Client
  Cultivations
Design Firm
  Bailey Design Group, Inc.
Designers
  David Fiedler, Lauren Dunoff, Tisha Armour, Christian Williamson

Client
Tom Douglas Restaurants

Design Firm
Walsh & Associates, inc.

Designers
Miriam Lisco, Jane Shasky

Client
Taylor Made Golf Co.

Design Firm
Laura Coe Design Assoc

Designer
Leanne Leveillee

Client
Xircom

Design Firm
McNulty & Co.

Creative Director and Designer
Jennifer McNulty

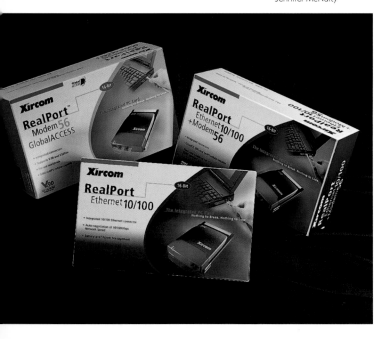

Client
Fresh Express

Design Firm
Full Steam Marketing & Design

Designer
Darryl Zimmerman

Client
   Bio Right International, Inc.

Design Firm
   Thompson Design Group

Designer
   Felicia Utomo

Client
   H.P. Hood, Inc.

Design Firm
   The Coleman Group

Client
   Target

Design Firm
   Hillis Mackey

Designer
   Terry Mackey

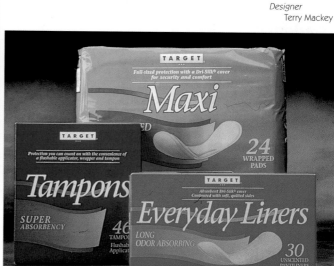

Client
   Interactive Learning Group

Design Firm
   Hedstrom/Blessing

Designer
   Pam Goebel

65

Client
Miracle Gro

Design Firm
Interbrand Gerstman + Meyers

Designers
Rafael Feliciano and Staff

Client
Compago Creative

Design Firm
Compago Creative

Designer and Illustrator
Sandra Pirie-St. Amour

Client
Charms

Design Firm
Harbauer Price Nelson Design

Designers
Harbauer Price Nelson Design Creative Team

Client
Life Uniform

Design Firm
CUBE Advertising & Design

Designer
David Chiow

Client
  Lotte Korea
Design Firm
  Cassata & Associates
Designers
  James Wolfe, Lesley Wexler

Client
  Mirage Resorts for Bellagio
Design Firm
  Girvin
Art Director   *Graphic Designer*   *Illustrator*
  Stephen Pannone   Erich Schreck   Francis Livingston

Client
  Wild Bird Centers of America
Design Firm
  Icon Graphics, Inc.
Designers
  Icon Graphics, Inc.

Client
  Labatt USA Inc.
Design Firm
  HMS Design Inc.
Designer
  Paul Beichert

Client
    Peninsula Area Chamber of Commerce
Design Firm
    Herip Associates
Designers
    Walter Herip, Rick Holb

Client
    EVD Advertising
Design Firm
    EVD Advertising
Designers
    Rachel Deutsch, David Street

Client
    Procter & Gamble
Design Firm
    Interbrand Gerstman + Meyers
Designers
    Chris Sander, Christian Niedhard

Client
    Icicle Seafoods, Inc.
Design Firm
    Faine-Oller Productions, Inc.
Designers
    Catherine Oller, Barbara Faine

Client
State of Hawaii, Ocean Resources Branch

Design Firm
Eric Woo Design Inc.

Designers
Eric Woo, Neal Izumi, David Louie

Client
Cracker Barrel Old Country Store

Design Firm
Phoenix Creative, St. Louis

Designer   *Illustrator*
Steve Hicks   Mike Weaver

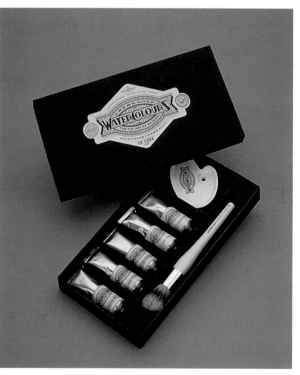

Client
General Mills

Design Firm
Compass Design

Designers
Mitchell Lindgren, Tom Arthur, Rich McGowen

Client
Gianna Rose

Design Firm
Sayles Graphic Design

Designer
John Sayles

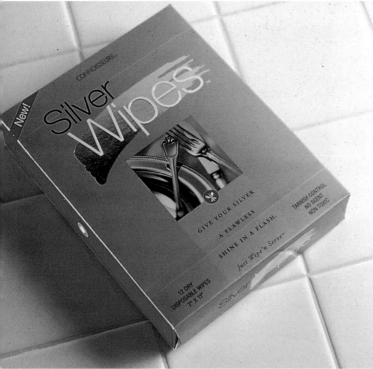

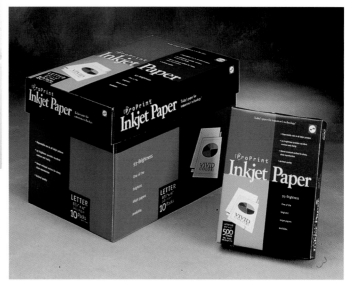

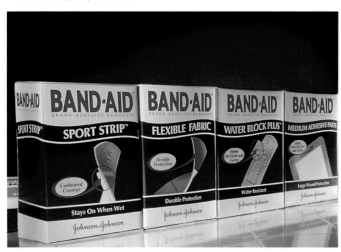

Client
    Casa Cuervo, S.A. de C.V.
Design Firm
    Klim Design, Inc.
Designer
    Matt Klim

Client
    MailStation
Design Firm
    Visigy
Designers
    Chris Ardito, Suzy Leung, Nicola Ginzler

Client
    C.F. Martin & Co.
Design Firm
    Bailey Design Group, Inc.
Designer
    Laura Markley

Client
    Broderbrund/The Learning Company
Design Firm
    Bruce Yelaska Design
Designer
    Bruce Yelaska

Client
   Time-Life Music
Design Firm
   Gold & Associates
Designers
   Joe Vavra, Keith Gold

Client
   Genesee Brewing Co.
Design Firm
   McElveney & Palozzi Design Group
Designers
   Matt Garrity, Matt Nowicki

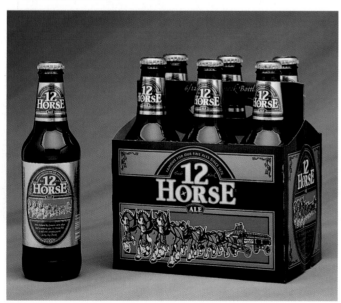

Client
   Suvinil
Design Firm
   Landor Associates
Designer
   Andy Johnson

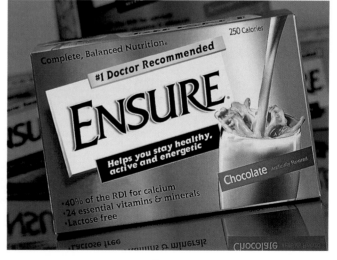

Client
   Ross Products Division, Abbot Laboratories
Design Firm
   Harbauer Bruce Nelson Design
Designer
   Craig Harbauer

72

Client
  Hanes
Design Firm
  Landor Associates
Designer
  Jerry Solon

Client
  Taylor Made
Design Firm
  Wallace Church
Designers
  Nin Glaister, Paula Bunny

Client
  Kemps
Design Firm
  Compass Design
Designers
  Mitchell Lindgren, Tom Arthur, Rich McGowen

Client
  Target
Design Firm
  Hillis Mackey
Designer
  Randy Szarzynski

Client
　Alonti Cafe

Design Firm
　NY ☆ LA, Inc.

Designers
　Kathryn M. Hardin, Angela R. Bartuska

Client
　Target Packaging

Design Firm
　Baker Associates

Creative Director　　　　Art Directors
　Scott Baker　　　　　Christopher Everett, Julie Lyrek

Designers
　Greg Preslicka, Christine Anderson, Julie Hinds,
　Mike Tophen, Mike Langer, Vic Ziolkowski

Client
　Brown Forman

Design Firm
　Abney/Huninghake Design Group

Designer
　Doreen Dehart

Client
　Compass Group of America

Design Firm
　Bailey Design Group, Inc.

Designer
　Steve Perry

Client
  Tully's Coffee Company

Design Firm
  Werkhaus Creative Communications

Designers
  Julie Poth, Steve Barrett, Teresa Forrester, Lynette Bradbury

Client
  Nova Wines Inc.

Design Firm
  Ortega Design Studio

Designer
  Susann Ortega

Client
  Lander Company

Design Firm
  Interbrand Gerstman + Meyers

Designers
  Rafael Feliciano and Staff

Client
  Westwood Studios

Design Firm
  Creative Dynamics

Designers
  Eddie Roberts, Victoria Hart

75

Client
Friskies Pet Care Co., Inc.

Design Firm
Thompson Design Group

Designers
Elizabeth Berta, Dennis Thompson

Client
W.F. Young

Design Firm
Luis R. Lee & Associates

Designers
Luis R. Lee, Heather Van Loan

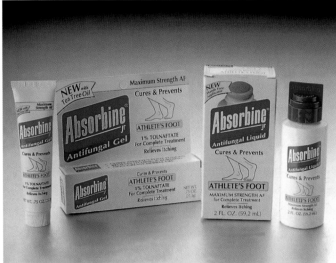

Client
Kemps

Design Firm
Hillis Mackey

Designer
Randy Szarzynski

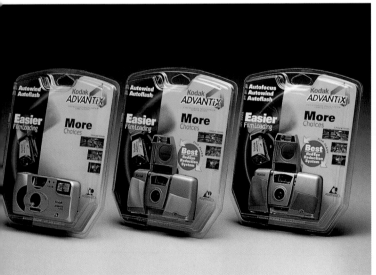

Client
Eastman Kodak Company

Design Firm
McElveney & Palozzi Design Group Inc.

Designers
Steve Palozzi, Jon Westfall

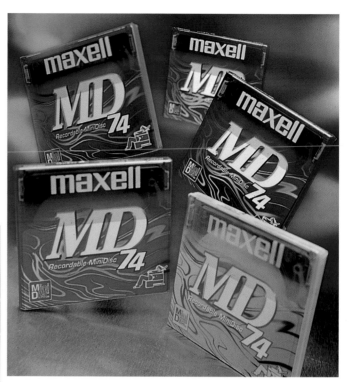

Client
  K2 Inline Skates

Design Firm
  Werkhaus Creative Communications

Designers
  Julie Poth, Teresa Forrester, James Sundstad

Client
  The Maxell Corporation of America

Design Firm
  Bailey Design Group, Inc.

Designer
  Denise Bosler

Client
  Snap-on Tool Corporation

Design Firm
  Design North, Inc.

Designer
  Pat Cowan

Client
  H.P. Hood, Inc.

Design Firm
  Hughes Design

Client
  Bath & Body Works
Design Firm
  Landor Associates
Designers
  Jeremy Dawkins, Pippa White

Client
  Nestlé USA—Chocolate & Confections
Design Firm
  Thompson Design Group
Designer
  Dave Dzurek

Client
  DeLorme Inc.
Design Firm
  LMS Design
Designers
  Richard Shear, Alex Williams

Client
  Quaker Oats Company
Design Firm
  Haugaard Creative Group Inc.
Designer
  Robert Pearson

Client
Cha Cha Beauty Parlor

Design Firm
Planet Design Co.

Designer
Dan Ibarra

Client
Tubby's

Design Firm
FCS, Inc.

Designers
Frank Fisher, Shana Mueller

Client
Sticky Fingers Bakery

Design Firm
Hornall Anderson Design Works

Designers
Jana Nishi, Sonja Max

Client
Durex

Design Firm
Landor Associates

Designer
Jeremy Dawkins

Client
Vitrex Gourmet Group

Design Firm
Goldforest

Designer
David Forest

Client
William Grant & Sons

Design Firm
Bailey Design Group, Inc.

Designer
Gary LaCroix

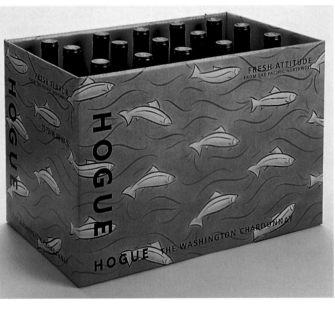

Client
Milos Restaurant

Design Firm
Landor Associates

Designer
Robert Matza

Client
VINTAGE NEW WORLD, Hogue Cellars

Design Firm
Walsh & Associates, inc.

Designers
Lyn Blanchard, Miriam Lisco, Jane Shasky

Client
Albertson's

Design Firm
Landor Associates

Designer
Alice Coxe

Client
Kaytee Products, Inc.

Design Firm
Design North, Inc.

Designer
Pat Cowan

Client
Kendall Creative Shop

Design Firm
Kendall Creative Shop

Designer
Mark K. Platt

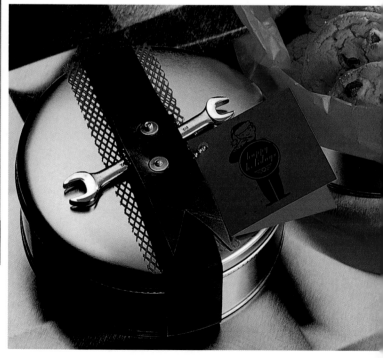

Client
Kemps

Design Firm
Compass Design

Designers
Mitchell Lindgren, Tom Arthur, Rich McGowan

81

Client
    Timeworks, Inc.

Design Firm
    Kowalski Design Works, Inc.

Designer
    Carrie Wallahan

Client
    Unilever HPC

Design Firm
    R. Bird & Co.

Designers
    Joe Favata, Michele Li

Client
    Clif Bar

Design Firm
    Visigy

Designers
    Linda Kelley, Suzy Leung, Nicola Ginzler

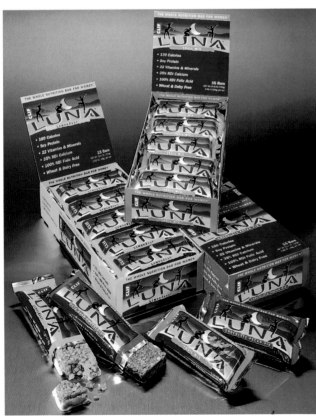

Client
    Heinz Frozen Foods

Design Firm
    Design North, Inc.

Designers
    Gwen Granzow, Jackie Langenecker

Client
Gardetto

Design Firm
Design North, Inc.

Designers
Pat Cowan, Jane Marcussen, Gwen Granzow

Client
Schroeder & Tremayne

Design Firm
Wallace Church

Designers
Wendy Church, Paula Bunny

Client
Best Foods

Design Firm
R. Bird & Company

Designer
Joe Favata

Client
Garden Valley Microwave Foods

Design Firm
Hillis Mackey

Designer
Terri Gray

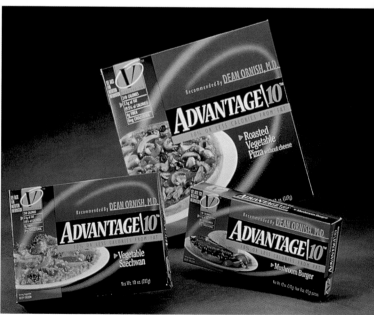

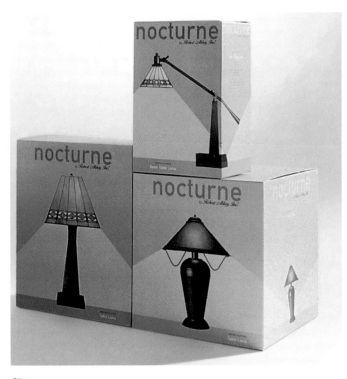

Client
Target Stores

Design Firm
Design Guys

Art Director
Steven Sikora

Designer
Amy Kirkpatrick

Client
Ray O Vac

Design Firm
Zen Design Group

Designer
David Perrin

Client
The Learning Company

Design Firm
SBG Enterprise

Designers
Thomas Bond, Iraxte Mumford

Client
Glazed Expressions

Design Firm
Sayles Graphic Design

Designer
John Sayles

Client
Fishery Products International

Design Firm
Forward

Designers
Forward

Client
Van de Kamp's

Design Firm
SBG Enterprise

Designers
Mark Bergman, Phillip Ting

Client
Naturally Vitamin

Design Firm
Icon Graphics, Inc.

Designers
Icon Graphics, Inc.

Client
Hewlett Packard

Design Firm
Laura Coe Design Assoc

Designer
Leanne Leveillee

85

Client
    Dunkin Donuts
Design Firm
    Design Forum
Designers
    Vivienne Padilla, Brent Beck

Client
    Newman's Own Inc.
Design Firm
    Zunda Design Group

Creative Director
    Charles Zunda
Designer
    John Voss

Client
    Intelliguard
Design Firm
    Dickson Design

Client
    H.P. Hood, Inc.
Design Firm
    The Coleman Group

Client
   Life Uniform
Design Firm
   Cube Advertising & Design
Designer
   David Chiow

Client
   Triarc Beverage Group
Design Firm
   HMS Design, Inc.
Designer
   Kim Kelse

Client
   Angostura International
Design Firm
   Klim Design, Inc.
Designer
   Matt Klim

Client
   Pearl Izumi
Design Firm
   Phoenix Creative, St. Louis
Designer
   Steve Wienke

Client
  Starbucks

Design Firm
  Werkhaus Creative Communications

Designers
  Christina Stein, John Burgess

Client
  Allied Signal Consumer Products

Design Firm
  HMS Design, Inc.

Designer
  Mary Ellen Butkus

Client
  Sony

Design Firm
  Handler Design Group

Designer
  Bruce Handler

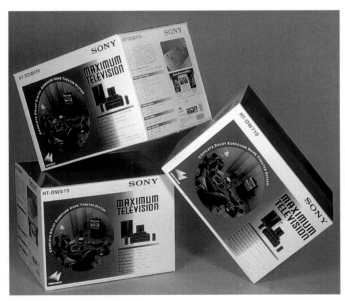

Client
  Schramsberg Winery

Design Firm
  Ortega Design Studio

Designers
  Susann Ortega, Joann Ortega

Client
Student Work (Class Project)

Design Firm
Lee, Eunju (graduate student at Pratt Inst.)

Designer
Lee, Eunju

Client
Cadbury Beverages, Inc.

Design Firm
SBG Enterprise

Designers
Mark Bergman, Jessie McAnulty

Client
Best Foods

Design Firm
Wallace Church

Designers
Joe Cuticone, Wendy Church

Client
Great American Audio

Design Firm
Zunda Design Group

Creative Director
Charles Zunda

Art Director
Todd Nickel

89

Client
  Kaytee Products Inc.

Design Firm
  Design North, Inc.

Designers
  Gwen Granzow, Jackie Langenecker

Client
  Newman's Own Inc.

Design Firm
  Zunda Design Group

Creative Director   Designer
  Charles Zunda   Jon Voss

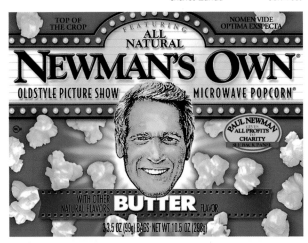

Client
  Simi Winery

Design Firm
  Ortega Design Sutdio

Designers
  Joann Ortega, Susann Ortega

Client
  Excel Corp.

Design Firm
  SBG Enterprise

Designer
  Mark Bergman

Client
Karbiz Associates

Design Firm
Eric Woo Design Inc.

Designer
Eric Woo

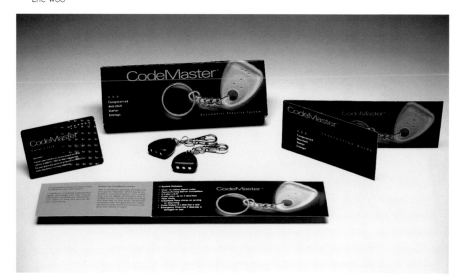

Client
Playtex Products

Design Firm
Zunda Design Group

Creative Director
Charles Zunda

Art Director
Paul Laplaca

Designers
Todd Nickel, Jon Voss

Client
SKF

Design Firm
Interbrand Gerstman + Meyers

Designers
Mitch Gottlieb, Christian Niedhard

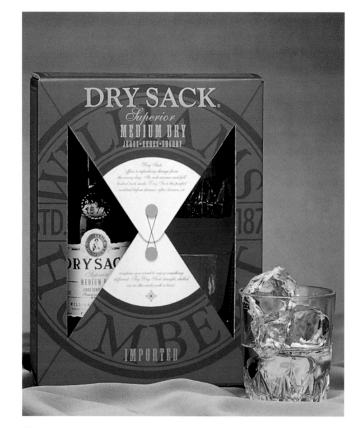

Client
William Grant & Sons

Design Firm
Bailey Design Group, Inc.

Designer
Steve Perry

91

Client
Pawel & Paul's

Design Firm
Hunt Weber Clark Assoc., Inc.

Designers
Nancy Hunt-Weber, Jim Deeken, Robin Snicer

Client
Venture Stores

Design Firm
Phoenix Creative, St. Louis

Designer
Ed Mantels-Seeker

Client
First Brands

Design Firm
Interbrand Gerstman + Meyers

Designers
Jeff Zack, Larry Riddell

Client
FPC Inc., A Kodak Company

Design Firm
Poonja Design

Designer
Suleman Poonja

Client
  General Mills

Design Firm
  Hillis Mackey

Designer
  Kelly Esterby

Client
  Borders Group, Inc.

Design Firm
  Phoenix Creative, St. Louis

Designer
  Susan Binns-Roth

Client
  Pamela's Product

Design Firm
  Dickson Design

Designer
  Deborah Shea

Client
  Canandaigua Wine Company

Design Firm
  Forward

Designer
  Brenda Benedict

Client
Del Monte Foods

Design Firm
SBG Enterprise

Designer
Mark Bergman

Client
Nikola's European Specialties

Design Firm
Compass Design

Designers
Mitchell Lindgren, Tom Arthur, Rich McGowen

Client
Bath & Body Works

Design Firm
Design Guys

Art Director
Steven Sikora

Designers
Anne Peterson, Gary Patch, Steven Sikora

Client
Kids II

Design Firm
Wages Design

Designer
Matt Taylor

LETTERHEAD DESIGNS

ELIAS|SAVION
INTER@CTIVE

Client
   Elias/Savion Advertising
Design Firm
   Elias/Savion Advertising
Designers
   Ronnie Savion, Philip Elias

▼
2 4 4 0
CNG TOWER
PITTSBURGH
PENNSYLVANIA
1 5 2 2 2
•
412. 642.7700
—
F   A   X
412. 642.2277
@
W W W
elias-savion.com

Viva il Vino!
A Wine, Gifts & Getaways Auction

HONORARY BOARD

John W. Barton, Sr., *Chair*

Mary Kay Brown

Dudley W. Coates

Paula Pennington de la Bretonne

Gov. and Mrs. M.J. "Mike" Foster, Jr.

Alice Greer

Lane Grigsby

Cole Jennings

Nanette Noland Kelley

Charles W. Lamar III

Richard A. Lipsey

C. Brent McCoy

Ben R. Miller, Jr.

Markham McKnight

Jake L. Netterville

John B. Noland

Dr. Huel D. Perkins

Miles Pollard, Jr.

Gordon A. Pugh

Kevin Reilly, Jr.

Mary Ann Sternberg

Thomas H. Turner

Mike Wampold

Milton J. Womack

POST OFFICE BOX 2992 • BATON ROUGE, LA 70821 • SPONSORED BY FORUM 35

Client
   Forum 35
Design Firm
   DSI/LA
Designer
   Nicole Duet

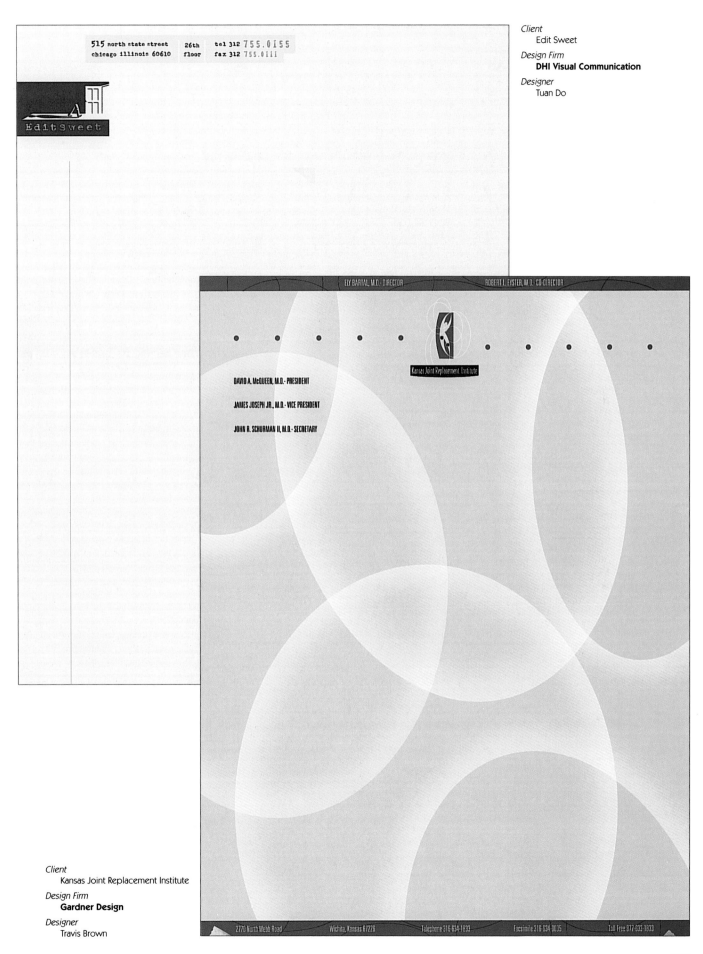

515 north state street 26th tel 312 755.0155
chicago illinois 60610 floor fax 312 755.0111

EditSweet

Client
Edit Sweet

Design Firm
DHI Visual Communication

Designer
Tuan Do

ELY BARTAL, M.D. - DIRECTOR   ROBERT L. EYSTER, M.D. - CO-DIRECTOR

Kansas Joint Replacement Institute

DAVID A. McQUEEN, M.D. - PRESIDENT

JAMES JOSEPH JR., M.D. - VICE PRESIDENT

JOHN R. SCHURMAN II, M.D. - SECRETARY

2770 North Webb Road   Wichita, Kansas 67226   Telephone 316-634-1833   Facsimile 316-634-0005   Toll Free 877-633-1833

Client
Kansas Joint Replacement Institute

Design Firm
Gardner Design

Designer
Travis Brown

7995 E. Prentice Ave., Suite 106
Englewood, CO 80111

FN 303.770.0114
FX 303.770.1201
TOLL FREE 1.877.994.2787

w w w . o p e n a r t s h o w . c o m

Client
   Open Art Show
Design Firm
   X Design Company
Designers
   Alex Valderrama, Amy Adams

blu print
COMMUNICATIONS

5580 Stapleton Drive • Atlanta, Georgia 30338
T 770.396.5156 • F 770.399.6969 • E dshelton@blueprintcom.com

Client
   Blue Print Communications
Design Firm
   Yellow Couch
Designers
   James Christian, Allison Cottrill

231 Milwaukee Street • Denver CO 80206   T 303-882-1269 • F 303-333-1711 • E ASIDIA@aol.com

Client
  The Manhattan Grill
Design Firm
  Ellen Bruss Design
Designers
  Jason C. Otero, Ellen Bruss

RIVERSIDE
STAGE
COMPANY

P.O. Box 253

Wilton,

Connecticut

06897-0253

203-762-8130

203-762-9384

www.riversidestageco.com

Client
  Riverside Stage Company
Design Firm
  Zunda Design Group
Designer
  Charles Zunda

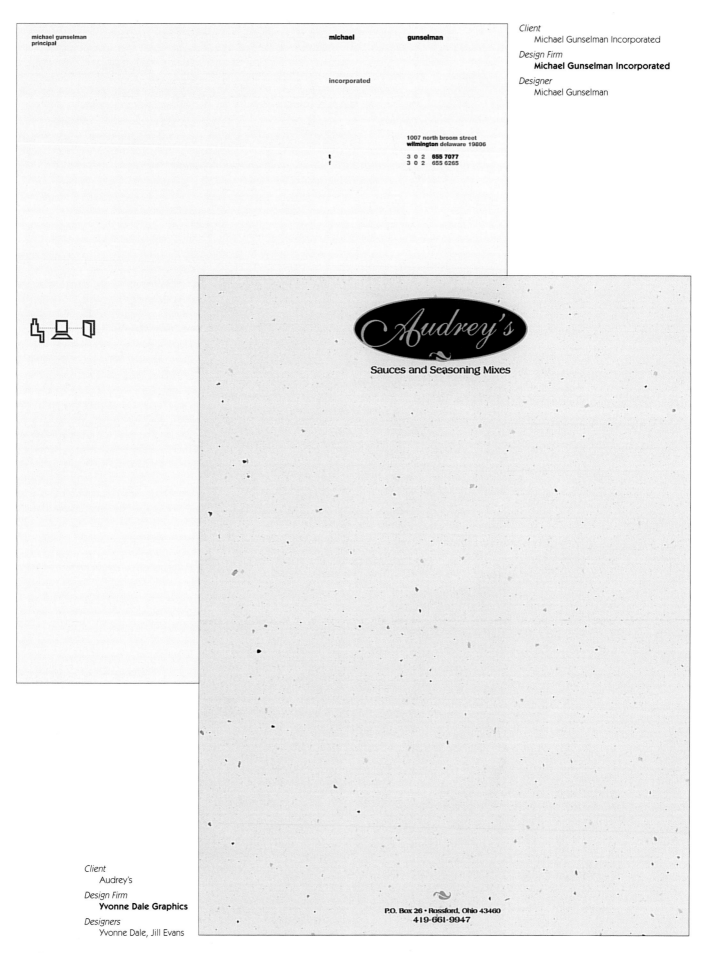

michael gunselman
principal

michael   **gunselman**

incorporated

1007 north broom street
wilmington delaware 19806
t   3 0 2 **655 7077**
f   3 0 2 655 6265

Client
Michael Gunselman Incorporated

Design Firm
Michael Gunselman Incorporated

Designer
Michael Gunselman

Audrey's
Sauces and Seasoning Mixes

P.O. Box 26 • Rossford, Ohio 43460
419-661-9947

Client
Audrey's

Design Firm
Yvonne Dale Graphics

Designers
Yvonne Dale, Jill Evans

Slow Cooked • Easy to Prepare • Marinated • Great Tasting

PO Box 2519 Wichita, KS 67201

Client
Excel

Design Firm
Gardner Design

Designer
Brian Miller

5207 Grant Avenue   Cleveland, Ohio 44125
t 216 641-7148 f 216 641-7147 e info@eguana.com

Client
eguana.com

Design Firm
Design Room

Designers
Chad Gordon, Kevin Rathge

Client
  Hollywood Physical Therapy Associates
Design Firm
  Asylum
Designers
  Jim Shanman, Andrea Wynnyk

HOLLYWOOD PHYSICAL THERAPY ASSOCIATES

7080 Hollywood Boulevard . Suite 1015 . Hollyw

NUNLEY
CUSTOM HOMES

NUNLEY CUSTOM HOMES
2330 OLD MIDDLEFIELD WAY
SUITE NO. 10
MOUNTAIN VIEW, CA 94043 | t 650 390.9545
                          f 650 390.9546
                          e jnunley@aol.com

Client
  Nunley Custom Homes
Design Firm
  Michael Patrick Partners
Designers
  Brian Hilton, Connie Hwang
Design Director
  Dan O'Brien

Client
Radius Product Development
Design Firm
Arc Design
Designers
Jac Phillips, Kevin O'Leary,
Kenny Bergen, Todd Kinniburgh

203 Union Street, Clinton, MA 01510 • tel 97

825 Main St. > Buffalo, NY 14203 T > 716.961.0857 F > 716.961.0856

JOHN PETERS
PHOTOGRAPHY

Client
John Peters Photography
Design Firm
Crowley Webb And Associates
Designer
Dion Pender

ELITE
PROPERTIES

P.O. Box 3027, Hwy 14
T: 912-756-544

Life's a Ch²rm

13999 Aquilla Road   FX: 440 834.9078
Burton, Ohio 44021   PH: 440 834.0239
www.charmies.com   Toll Free: 877 528.1501

Home of Charmies Collectibles and Team Charmies

Client
  Elite Properties
Design Firm
  Hunter Advertising
Designer
  Carolyn J. Hunter

Client
  Life's A Charm
Design Firm
  Nesnadny + Schwartz
Designers
  Gregory Oznowich,
  Timothy Lachina, Stacie Ross

e EpicEdge™

Client
Epic Edge

Design Firm
Addison Whitney

Designer
Kimberlee Davis

SCRIP**MASTER**

toll free	800-444-8486
PHO	316 262-2231
FAX	262-5115

245 N. Waco, STE. 100
Wichita, Kansas 67202

PHARMACY
MANAGEMENT
SYSTEMS

Client
Scripmaster

Design Firm
Gardner Design

Designer
Brian Miller

WORLD OM DAY
a moment of reflection

Client
World OM Day
Design Firm
Spencer Zahn & Associates
Designers
Spencer Zahn, Joseph McCarthy,
Ed McHugh

WORLD OM DAY® SY
THIS MOMENT OF REFLECTI
112 WEST 34TH STREET, SUITE 920 • NEW YORK, NY 1012

grape finds

Client
Grapefinds
Design Firm
Hornall Anderson Design Works
Designers
Jack Anderson, Lisa Cerveny,
Gretchen Cook, Jana Wilson Esser,
Mary Chin Hutchison, Sonja Max,
Julia LaPine

CW Designs, Inc.

253 EAST AURORA ROAD
NORTHFIELD CENTER, OH 44067

PH: 330-467-3337

FX: 330-467-3385

Client
 CW Designs, Inc.

Design Firm
 Flourish

Designers
 Christopher Ferranti, Henry Frey

ART SPACE

H&R BLOCK ARTSPACE AT THE KANSAS CITY ART INSTITUTE

16 EAST 43RD STREET KANSAS CITY, MISSOURI 64111 • TEL: 816.561.5563 • FAX: 816.561.5993

Client
 The Kansas City Art Institute

Design Firm
 EAT Advertising & Design

Art Director, Designer
 DeAnne Dodd

Creative Director
 Patrice Jobe

108

Client
Houston Medical Research Associates
Design Firm
Marion Graphics, L.C.
Designer
Marion Graphics, L.C.

nQuest

800 Pe
Phone 281.893

www.naturalquestion.com

Client
Natural Question Technology
Design Firm
Blank—Robert Kent Wilson
Designer
Robert Kent Wilson

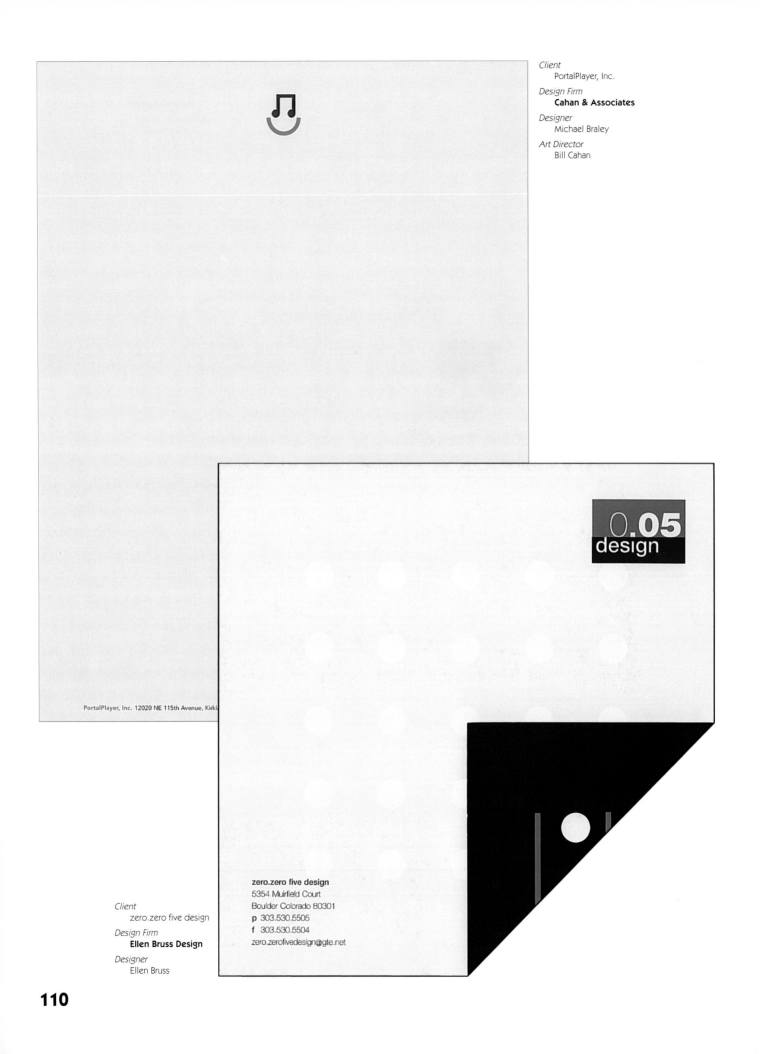

Client
  PortalPlayer, Inc.
Design Firm
  Cahan & Associates
Designer
  Michael Braley
Art Director
  Bill Cahan

PortalPlayer, Inc. 12020 NE 115th Avenue, Kirkl.

0.05
design

zero.zero five design
5354 Muirfield Court
Boulder Colorado 80301
p 303.530.5505
f 303.530.5504
zero.zerofivedesign@gte.net

Client
  zero.zero five design
Design Firm
  Ellen Bruss Design
Designer
  Ellen Bruss

CoinZone.com

The Collectors' Choice

PO Box 310
Warwick, NY 10990
P 914.986.6656
F 914.651.9088
E info@coinzone.com

Client
  CoinZone
Design Firm
  Barth and Co. Graphic Design
Designer
  Rob Barth

offices‹ chapel hill **I** princeton **I** new york

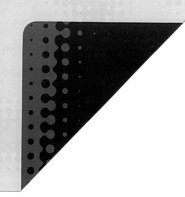

an **IBM** business partner

Client
  Telos Group
Design Firm
  Crowley Webb And Associates
Designer
  Dion Pender

111

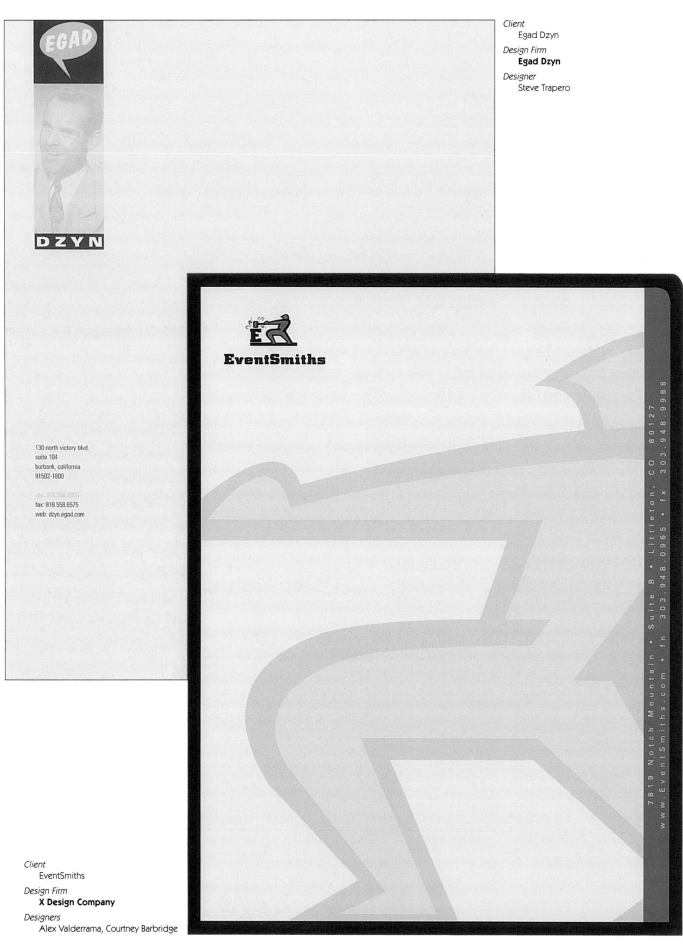

Client
Egad Dzyn
Design Firm
Egad Dzyn
Designer
Steve Trapero

130 north victory blvd.
suite 104
burbank, california
91502-1800

vox: 818.558.6988
fax: 818.558.6575
web: dzyn.egad.com

Client
EventSmiths
Design Firm
X Design Company
Designers
Alex Valderrama, Courtney Barbridge

112

Client
 Active Motif
Design Firm
 Laura Coe Design Assoc.
Designer
 Ryoichi Yotsumoto

5431-C Avenida Encinas
Carlsbad, CA 92008

760.431.1263 *ph*
760.431.1351 *fax*
www.activemoti*f*

150 Baker Avenue Extension
Concord, Massachusetts 01742

TEL 978•318•9981
FAX 978•318•9280

Client
 myteam.com
Design Firm
 Partners & Simons
Designer
 Anthony Henriques

Client
  Sozo
Design Firm
  Milligan Design
Designers
  Michael Milligan, Megan Ploska

S O Z O
ART + NATURE

FORTY - ONE
CENTRAL PARK WEST
NEW YORK, NY 10023

212.580.4091 TEL
212.580.0249 FAX

The University's Campaign for Hawai'i
Building Rainbow Bridges

University of Hawaii Foundation · PO BOX 11270 · Honolulu, Hawaii 96828-0270 · Tel (808) 956-8849 · Fax (808) 956-5115

Client
  University of Hawaii Foundation
Design Firm
  Eric Woo Design, Inc.
Designer
  Eric Woo

Client
  Big Bark Bakery
Design Firm
  Kendall Creative Shop
Designer
  Mark K. Platt

2538 Elm Street

Dallas, TX 75226

tel: 214.741.6173

fax: 214.742.6689

toll free: 888.3.BOWWOW

www.bigbarkbakery.com

Spellbound Creative Concepts, LLC
9080 Santa Monica Boulevard Los Angeles, CA 90069
Voice 310 860 0870 Facsimile 310 860 0873
www.SpellboundCreative.com

Client
  Spellbound Creative Concepts, LLC
Design Firm
  J. Robert Faulkner Advertising
Designer
  J. Robert Faulkner

digital realtor
WESTSIDE PROPERTIES

www.digitalrealtor.com   Tel: 310.577.80

Client
Digital Realtor
Design Firm
Poonja Design
Designer
Suleman Poonja

Client
Retail Results, Inc.
Design Firm
CUBE Advertising & Design
Designer
David Chiow

RETAIL RESULTS
314 434 7237

Client
PB&J Restaurants

Design Firm
EAT Advertising & Design

Art Director, Designer
DeAnne Dodd

Creative Director
Patrice Jobe

PRESIDENT,
PB&J RESTAURANTS
Paul Khoury

MANAGING DIRECTOR,
CULINARY CONCEPTS, LTD.
E. Tom Johnson

PRESIDENT, JLWLC
Roxanne Wu-Rebein

PRESIDENT-ELECT, JLWLC
Maureen Mahoney

GALA EVENT CO-CHAIRS
Jeanne Peterson
Alice Hawk

COOKING CLASS
EVENT CO-CHAIRS
Linda Sands
Amy Parker

THE JUNIOR LEAGUE
OF WYANDOTTE AND
JOHNSON COUNTIES
IN KANSAS, INC.

509 ARMSTRONG
P.O. BOX 17-1487
KANSAS CITY, KS 66117
913-371-2303

THE GUIDANCE CLINIC

A Center for
Children and Families

2615 Stadium Drive
Kalamazoo, MI 49008
(616) 343-1651
FAX (616) 382-7078

FAMILY RESOURCE CENTER • OUTPATIENT TESTING AND THERAPY • INFANT AND PARENT SERVICES • SUBSTANCE ABUSE COUNSELING

Client
The Guidance Clinic

Design Firm
LKF Marketing

Designers
Sue Severeid, Rene Rodriguez

*apple*designsource inc.
global strategic branding & package design

160 madison avenue, new york NY 10016
t: 212.252.9115 f: 212.252.9117
www.appledesignsource.com

Client
apple designsource inc.

Design Firm
apple designsource inc.

PREVAIL

THINKING SKILLS THAT FACILITATE INNOVATION.   P. O. Box 100 Marietta, GA 30061-0100

T] 770 426 1008   F] 770 420 8001   www.prevail.org

Client
Prevail

Design Firm
Wages Design

Designer
Joanna Tak

118

GlobalCable CONSULTING GROUP

Management support and
information technology solutions
cable TV worldwide

4915 Saint Elmo Avenue · Suite 403

newenergy

Client
  Global Cable Consulting Group
Design Firm
  Tim Kenney Design Partners
Designer
  Marica Banko
Creative Director
  Tim Kenney

Client
  NewEnergy
Design Firm
  Cahan & Associates
Designers
  Michael Braley, Ben Pham
Art Director
  Bill Cahan

119

CLEAR *INSIGHT*
Extraordinary Communication Enablers

Client
Clear Insight

Design Firm
Clear Insight

Designer
Julie Eubanks

Atlanta
260 Interstate North Circle, NW
Atlanta, Georgia 30339-2111
Telephone 770.763.1000
Facsimile 770.859.4403

Miami
11222 Quail Roost Drive
Miami, Florida 33157-6596
Telephone 305.253.2244
Facsimile 305.252.6987

Internet: www.assurant.com

Assurant*Group*℠

FORTIS
Solid partners, flexible solutions℠

Assurant is part of the Fortis group

Client
Assurant Group

Design Firm
Wages Design

Designer
Matt Taylor

McGRANAHAN architects

950 Fawcett, Suite 300 Tacoma, Washington 98402

253 383 3084 T
253 383 3097 F

www.mcgranahan.com

Client
McGranahan Architects
Design Firm
The Traver Company
Designers
Christopher Downs, Dale Hart

1216 Dormont Avenue   Suite Number One   Pittsburgh, PA 15216   t 412.531.2597   f 412.531.1218   l.l.kirchner@worldnet.att.net

communications

Client
Lisa Kirschner Communications
Design Firm
A to Z communications, inc.
Designer
Vonnie Hornburg

CEPTYR™

Client
    CEPTYR, Inc.
Design Firm
    9A Design
Designer
    Kurt Niedermeier

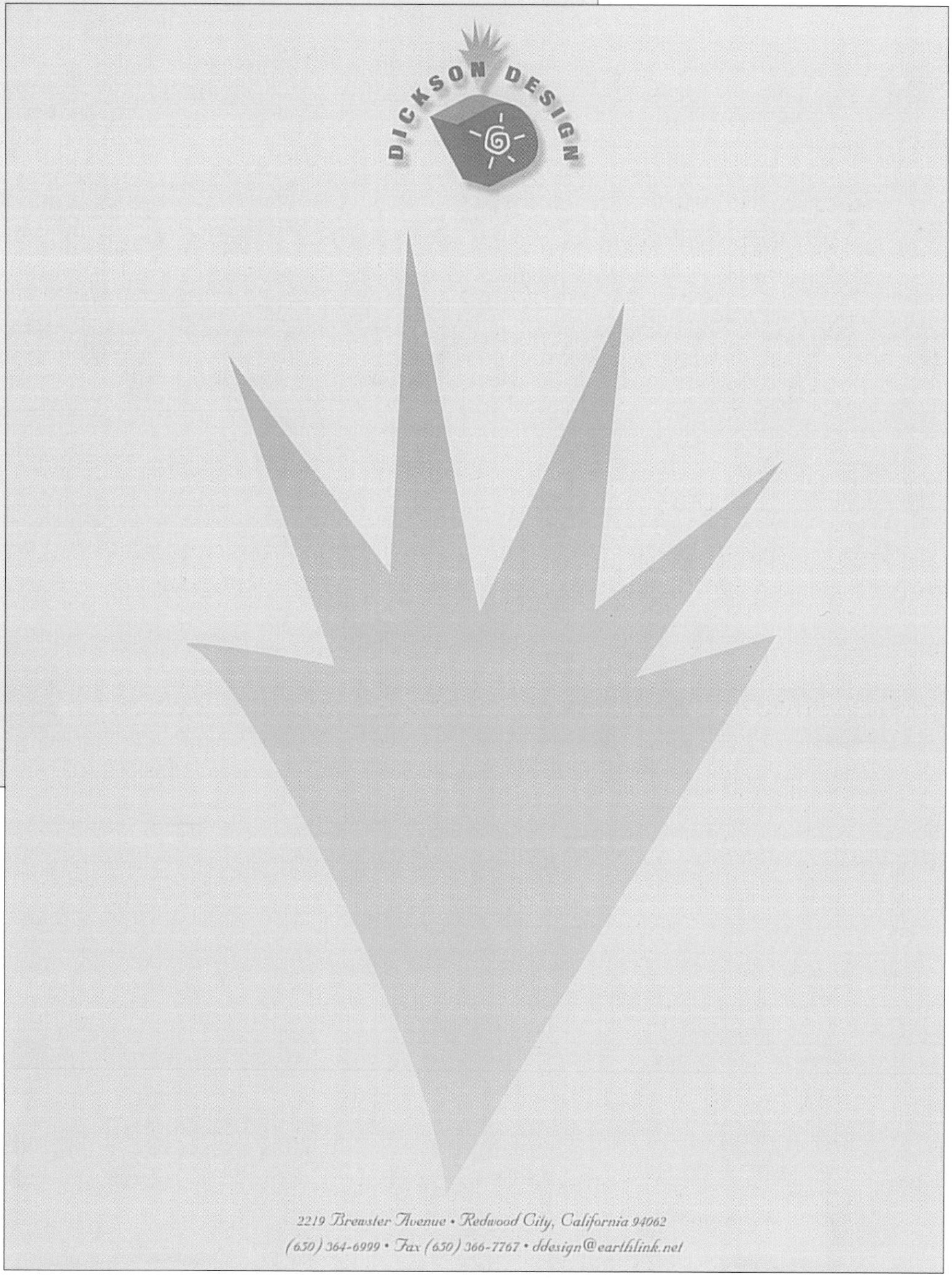

DICKSON DESIGN

2219 Brewster Avenue • Redwood City, California 94062
(650) 364-6999 • Fax (650) 366-7767 • ddesign@earthlink.net

Client
    Dickson Design
Design Firm
    Dickson Design
Designer
    Deborah Shea

Acadio Corporation
311B Occidental Ave. S.
Suite 200
Seattle WA 98104

Acadio

tel 206.225.5000 · fax 206.225.5099 · www.acadio

Client
Acadio Corporation
Design Firm
Werkhaus Creative Communications
Designers
Thad Boss, James Sundstad

Costanoa

P.O. Box 842   2001 Costanoa Road at Hwy 1, Pescadero, CA 94060   650.879.1100   fax 650.879.2275   reservations 800.738.7477
www.costanoa.com

Client
Joie de Vivre Hospitality
Design Firm
Hunt Weber Clark Assoc., Inc.
Designers
Christine Chung, Nancy Hunt-Weber

Client
Eventra
Design Firm
Tom Fowler, Inc.
Designer
Karl S. Maruyama

Client
Bouchard Marketing
Design Firm
Winter Graphics North
Designers
Simon Bishop-Olney, Derek Hocking

www.atpos.com | 500 Oakmead Parkway, Sunnyvale, California 94086 U.S.A.
t 408.524.4700 f 408.524.4299

@pos.com

IDEAS. PRINT+INTERACTIVE.

FUSE

775 Laguna Canyon Road
Laguna Beach, CA 92651   949 3760438
fax: 949 3760498   WWW.GOFUSE.COM

Client
@pos.com

Design Firm
Michael Patrick Partners

Design Director
Darice Koziel

Designers
Connie Hwang, Victoria Pohlmann

Client
Fuse

Design Firm
Fuse

Designer
Russell Pierce

125

Client
  The Axis Group, llc
Design Firm
  Wallace Church associates, inc.
Designers
  Stan Church, Wendy Church

AXIS

CAMPIELLO

Client
  D'Amico & Partners
Design Firm
  Little & Company
Designer
  Kathy Soranno
Design Director
  Jim Jackson

1320 West Lake Street ❧ Minneapolis, MN. 55408 ❧ Tel. (612) 825-2222 ❧ Fax. (612) 825-2162

126

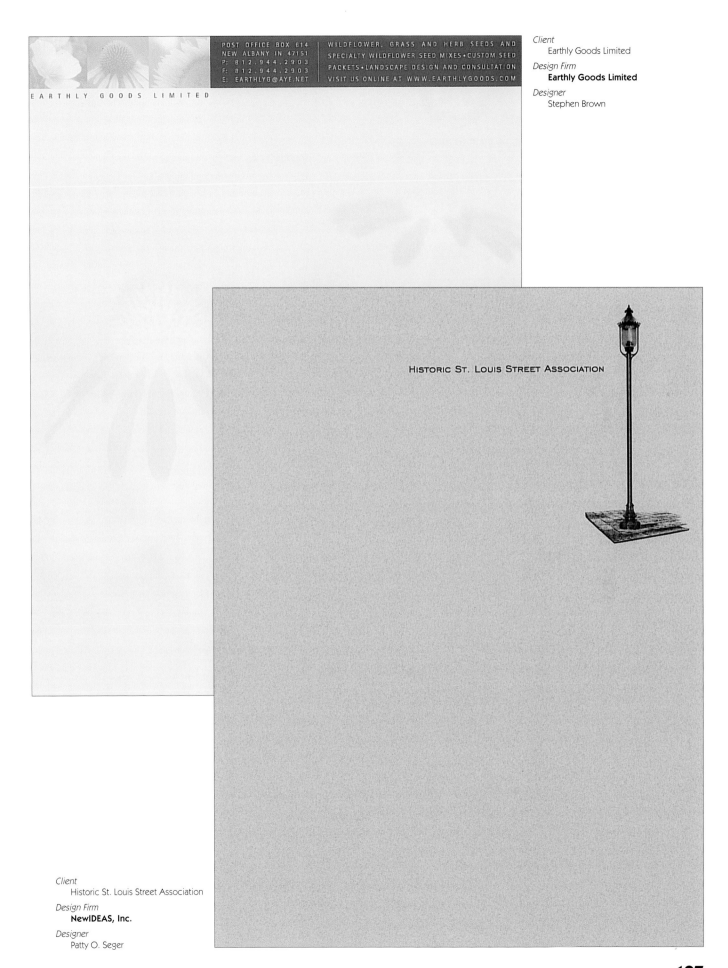

POST OFFICE BOX 614
NEW ALBANY IN 47151
P: 812.944.2903
F: 812.944.2903
E: EARTHLYG@AYE.NET

WILDFLOWER, GRASS AND HERB SEEDS AND
SPECIALTY WILDFLOWER SEED MIXES•CUSTOM SEED
PACKETS•LANDSCAPE DESIGN AND CONSULTATION
VISIT US ONLINE AT WWW.EARTHLYGOODS.COM

EARTHLY GOODS LIMITED

Client
Earthly Goods Limited
Design Firm
Earthly Goods Limited
Designer
Stephen Brown

HISTORIC ST. LOUIS STREET ASSOCIATION

Client
Historic St. Louis Street Association
Design Firm
NewIDEAS, Inc.
Designer
Patty O. Seger

127

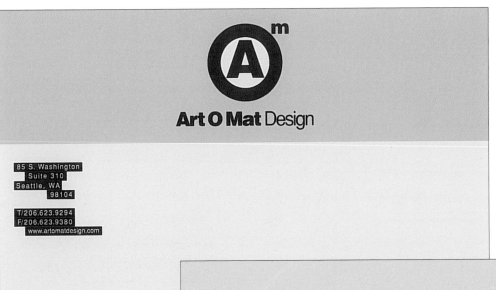

Client
Art O Mat Design

Design Firm
Art O Mat Design

Designers
Jacki McCarthy, Mark Kaufman

Art O Mat Design

85 S. Washington
Suite 310
Seattle, WA
98104

T/206.623.9294
F/206.623.9380
www.artomatdesign.com

CYND
SNOWBOARD APPAREL

33 MIMOSA COURT
QUAKERTOWN, PA
18951

215.538.3454
www.cynd.com

Client
CYND Snowboard Apparel

Design Firm
Visual Marketing Associates, Inc.

Designer
Jason Selke

ZEHNDER DESIGN COLLABORATIVE

413 Sixth Street • Shelbyville, KY •

Client
  Zehnder Design Collaborative
Design Firm
  Abney/Huninghake Design Group
Designers
  Karen Abney, Stephen Brown

g

green

media cultivation
8 Glen Road
Wayne, NJ 07470
Tel: 973 584 7193
info@greenmc.com
www.greenmc.com

Client
  Green Media Cultivation
Design Firm
  Wallace Church associates, inc.
Designers
  Nin Glaister, Paula Bunny

FORWARD
branding and identity

Client
  Forward
Design Firm
  Forward
Designer
  Daphne Stofer

1115 East Main Street

H O L Y

T R I N I T Y

C A T H O L I C

C H U R C H

1787 Anno Domini

3513 N ST. NW,
WASHINGTON,
D C   2 0 0 0 7

PH 202-337-2840
FX 202-337-9048

Client
  Holy Trinity Catholic Church
Design Firm
  Tim Kenney Design Partners
Creative Director, Designer
  Tim Kenney

Client
Beauchamp Group

Design Firm
Beauchamp Group

Designers
David Hintgen, Errol Beauchamp

beauchamp)group

1743 WAZEE SUITE 321
DENVER, CO 80202
T: 303.296.1133
BEAUCHAMPGRO

@RISK
SolutionsThroughDataMining

web www.atRiskInc.com e-mail Info@atRiskInc.com   1205 Westlakes Drive Suite 180 · Berwyn · PA · 19312   Tel · 610.296.0800   Fax · 610.296.8181

Client
@Risk, Inc.

Design Firm
LF Banks + Associates

Designers
Lori F. Banks, John German

131

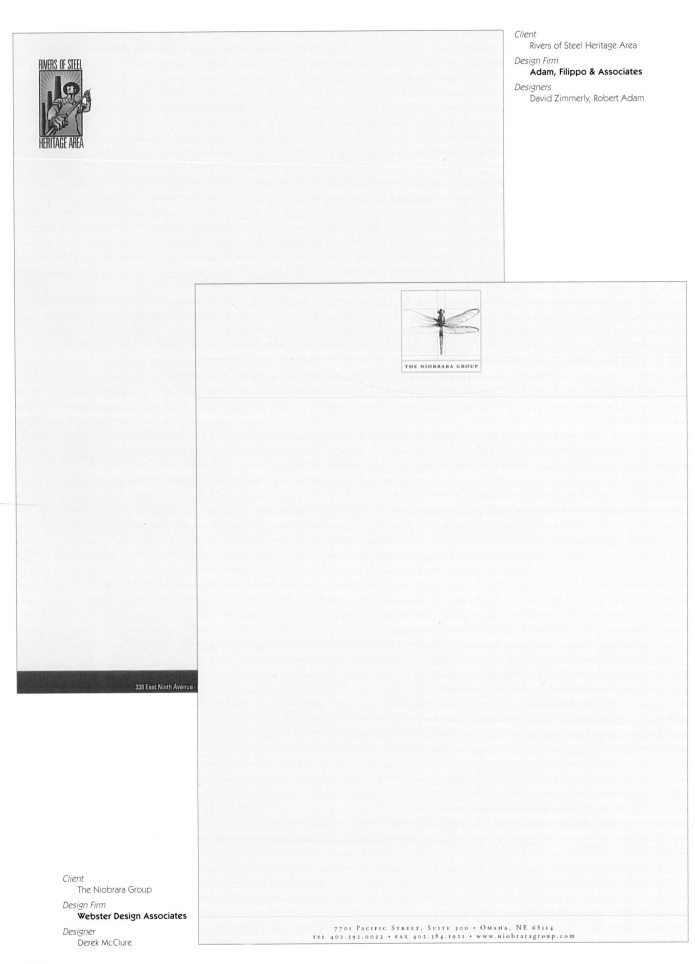

Client
Rivers of Steel Heritage Area
Design Firm
Adam, Filippo & Associates
Designers
David Zimmerly, Robert Adam

RIVERS OF STEEL
HERITAGE AREA

338 East Ninth Avenue ·

THE NIOBRARA GROUP

7701 PACIFIC STREET, SUITE 300 · OMAHA, NE 68114
TEL 402.392.0022 · FAX 402.384.1921 · www.niobraragroup.com

Client
The Niobrara Group
Design Firm
Webster Design Associates
Designer
Derek McClure

Client
   The Marketing Store
Design Firm
   The Marketing Store
Designer
   Susan Leeson

THE ELLIOTT

721 Pine Street
Seattle, WA 98101
t 206.262.0700
f 206.625.1221
www.elliotthotel.com

A HEDREEN HOTEL

Client
   R.C. Hedreen
Design Firm
   The Traver Company
Designer
   Margo Sepanski

Steelcase

Steelcase Inc., P.O.

STEREO
HK
HEST&KRAMER

Client
Steelcase, Inc.
Design Firm
Genesis, Inc.
Designers
Jim Adler, Dave Shelton, Dasha Hesker

HI-FIDELITY
5250 WEST 74TH STREET MINNEAPOLIS MINNESOTA 55439
TELEPHONE 612 831-3266 FACSIMILE 612 831-4105
EMAIL ADDRESS: INFO@HESTKRAMER.COM

Client
Hest & Kramer
Design Firm
Design Guys
Designer
Scott Thares
Art Director
Steven Sikora

134

3773 Cherry Creek Dr. North, Suite 575 · Denver, CO 80209 · Tel: 303-331-6425 · Fax: 303-331-3408

Client
Crescent Club
Design Firm
Schwener Design Group
Designers
Cynthia Brown, Diane Schwener

Client
Christine Kempter
Design Firm
H2D
Art Director
Joseph Hausch

Client
  The Washington Opera
Design Firm
  M-Art
Designer
  Marty Ittner

Plácido Domingo
Artistic Director

Patricia L. Mossel
Executive Director

Mrs. Stuart A. Bernstein
Gala Co-Chairman

Mrs. A. Huda Farouki
Gala Co-Chairman

The Washington Opera
2600 Virginia Avenue, NW
Suite 104
Washington, DC 20037
202/295-2486
FAX 202/295-2479

Client
  DuClaw Brewing Co.
Designer
  Alain Bolduc
Design Firm
  Gr8
Art Director
  Lisa Wurfl-Roeca

Client
Interactive Learning Group
Design Firm
Hedstrom/Blessing Inc.
Designer
Mike Goebel

INTERACTIVE LEARNING GROUP

5001 W. 80th Street, Suite 310
Bloomington, MN 55437
612-820-0600 *phone*
612-820-4650 *fax*

Fowler Bros., Inc. 10273 Lummisville Road   Wolcott, New York 14590 USA
315-594-8068   Fax: 315-594-8060   www.fowlerfarms.com

Client
Fowler Farms
Design Firm
McElveney & Palozzi Design Group Inc.
Designers
Matt Nowicki, William McElveney

137

innoVentry

Client
Wells Fargo
Design Firm
Hornall Anderson Design Works
Designers
Jack Anderson, Kathy Saito,
Alan Copeland

1650 TRIBUTE RD.
SACRAMENTO CA
95815-4400

(510) 843-5555

FifthStreetdesign

1250 Addison Street
Studio H
Berkeley
California
94702
idesign@fifthstreet.com

fax (510) 843-1505

Client
Fifth Street Design
Design Firm
Fifth Street Design
Designers
Brenton Beck, J. Clifton Meek

e_creative
copywriter

683 Calle Miramar
Redondo Beach, CA 90277

Phone 310 375 7855   Fax 310 375 6265   E-mail ecreative@earthlink.net

THE VERANDA
COLLECTION

188 MIDLAND AVENUE • POST OFFICE BOX 589 • BASALT, COLORADO 81621
PHONE 970-927-4466 • FAX 970-927-4477

Client
ecreative

Design Firm
Engle & Murphy

Designer
Robin Seaman

Client
The Veranda Collection

Design Firm
Schwener Design Group

Designer
Diane Schwener

139

www.pulseinc.com

Client
  Pulse Systems, Inc.
Design Firm
  Insight Design Communications
Designers
  Sherrie Holdeman, Tracy Holdeman

CORPORATE OFFICE • 3017 NORTH CYPRESS,

DELEO CLAY TILE COMPANY
MANUFACTURERS OF THROUGHBODY TILES

600 Chaney Street • Lake Elsinore • California • 92530
Telephone 909 674 1578 • 800 654 1119 • Fax 909 245 2427
www.deleoclaytile.com

Client
  Deleo Clay Tile Company
Design Firm
  Mires Design
Designers
  Jose Serrano, Dave Adey

140

CURLEY COMMUNICATIONS

1901 49th. Street
Sacramento, CA 95819

916.739.6575
916.739.6583 Fax
916.712.5116 Cell

Client
  Curley Communications
Design Firm
  Winter Graphics North
Designers
  Simon Bishop-Olney, Derek Hocking

Modula

2121 K Street, NW Washington, DC 20037   202.261.3590
202.261.3508 fax   RDBag@aol.com

Client
  Modula
Design Firm
  Blank—Robert Kent Wilson
Designer
  Robert Kent Wilson

über, inc.

über, inc • 231 west 29
tel 212.6

Client
Über, Inc.

Design Firm
Über, Inc.

Designers
Suzanne Jennerich, Herta Kriegner

Client
Greg Welsh Design

Design Firm
Greg Welsh Design

Designer
Greg Welsh

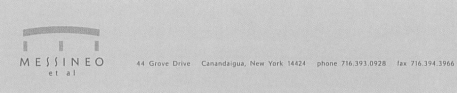

MESSINEO
et al

44 Grove Drive   Canandaigua, New York 14424   phone 716.393.0928   fax 716.394.3966

Client
Messineo et al

Design Firm
Icon Graphics, Inc.

Take Action For Our WILDWorld!

SAVM, LLC   210 Archer Street / Canton GA 30114   Ph: 888-945-3415 / Fx: 770-720-1546   wildweekend@mindspring.com

Client
Wild Weekend

Design Firm
**Environmental Communications
Associates, Inc.**

Designers
An Grant, Traci Schalow

143

haese ⊞ Limited Liability Company

haese

Attorneys at Law
70 Franklin Street, 9th Floor
Boston, Massachusetts 02110

Telephone 617.428.0266
Facsimile 617.428.0276
Web Site www.haese.com

100 Pearl Street, 14th Floor
Hartford, Connecticut 06103

Telephone 860.249.7194
Facsimile 860.249.7195

Attorneys also admitted to practice
in Colorado, Connecticut,
Rhode Island, New Hampshire,
New York and Washington, DC.

F ● C U S

design and marketing solutions

3800 VALLEYLIGHTS DRIVE
PASADENA, CA 91107

626 351-2046 TELEPHONE
626 351-8833 FAX

Client
  Haese, LLC

Design Firm
  Amisano Design

Designers
  Christine Amisano, Dianne Tine

Client
  FOCUS Design and
  Marketing Solutions

Design Firm
  **FOCUS Design and
  Marketing Solutions**

Designer
  Aram Youssefian

SALON
1520

1520 EASTLAKE AVE.

Client
   Evelyn Knoke
Design Firm
   Hansen Design Company
Designers
   Pat Hansen, Jacqueline Smith

★ FIELD ₀f DREAMS ★
FUTURE OF DIABETICS, INC.

2201 S. BREIEL BLVD. MIDDLETOWN, OH 45044
P.O.
BOX 4200

☎/937.623.9165
📠/740.852.0935

Client
   Future of Diabetics, Inc.
Design Firm
   Visual Marketing Associates, Inc.
Designer
   Jason Selke

ARCHITECTURAL & INTERIOR

DESIGN

NOTES:

1. STEVE HOWARD DESIGNS
   10606 DUNLAP
   HOUSTON, TEXAS 77096

2. FONE: 713-283-0777

3. FAX: 713-729-5691

Client
  Steve Howard Designs

Design Firm
  NY ☆ LA, Inc.

Designer
  Kathryn M. Hardin

Center
for Greater Philadelphia
University of Pennsylvania

Ted Hershberg
Director
Professor, Public Policy & History

CENTER FOR GREATER PHILADELPHIA   University of Pennsylvania   3701 Chestnut Street   6th Floor East   Philadelphia, PA 19104-3199
Phone: 215.898.8713   Fax: 215.898.9783   cgpinfo@pobox.upenn.edu   www.cgp.upenn.edu

Client
  Center for Greater Philadelphia

Design Firm
  LF Banks + Associates

Designers
  Lori F. Banks, John German

3 1 4
CLIFTON
AVENUE
MINNEAPOLIS
MN 55403
TEL 612 874 1415
FAX 612 874 1451

CHANGE INC

Client
   Change, Inc.
Design Firm
   William Homan Design
Designer
   William Homan

800 West Main Street ∷ Louisville, Kentucky 40202 ∷ 502 588 7228 ∷ 502 585 1179 Fax

Louisville Slugger Museum

Client
   Louisville Slugger Museum
Design Firm
   Abney/Huninghake Design Group
Designer
   Doreen Dehart

147

Client
  EAI
Design Firm
  EAI
Designers
  Todd Simmons,
  Matt Rollins, Phil Hamlett

⊢⟶

GEORGE ORLOFF, M.D., F.A.C.S.
Cosmetic and Reconstructive Surgery

EAI® 887 West Marietta St. NW J-101 Atlanta, Georg
404 875 8225 fax 875 0014 www.eai-atl.com

GEORGE ORLOFF, M.D., F.A.C.S. • 2701 W. ALAMEDA AVE., SUITE 401 • BURBANK, CA 91505 • 818.848.0590 • DRORLOFF@EARTHLINK.NET • WWW.DRORLOFF.COM

Client
  George Orloff, M.D.
Design Firm
  Glyphix Studio
Designer
  Eric Sena

INTERNATIONAL
GLASSMUSEUM

934 Broadway, Suite 204 Tacoma, Washington 98402 usa t 253 396 1768 f 253 396 1769

www.internationalg

PONTIO
COMMUNICATIONS
"Bridging the last mile"

Pontio Communications Company, Inc. • 1801 North Lamar, Suite M • Austin, TX 78701 • tel-512.485.7676 • fax-512.485.7235 • www.pontio.com

Client
International Glass Museum
Design Firm
The Traver Company
Designer
Christopher Downs

Client
Pontio Communications
Design Firm
Webster Design
Designers
Derek McClure, Dave Webster

THE
SUBWAY
ART OF
ROBERT
PADOVANO

ORIGINAL IMAGES
DEPICTING THE
NEW YORK SUBWAYS
AND THEIR SURROUNDING
ENVIRONMENT

One Purdy Avenue
Staten Island, New York 10314
tel. 718-494-0334
email: Rob2Peg@aol.com

Client
Robert Padovano

Design Firm
Robert Padovano Design

Designer
Robert Padovano

**Perennial
Homes**
Builder of the Complete Home

A Division of Saxton Incorporated

Saxton Incorporated • 5440 West Sahara Avenue, 3rd Floor • Las Vegas, Nevada 89146 • (702) 221-1111 • www.sxtn.com

Client
Saxton Incorporated

Design Firm
Creative Dynamics

Designers
Victor Rodriguez, Dawn Teagarden

S

SHEMRO Engineering

6902 West Avenue Bethesda, Maryland 20815

Phone 301.718.8113 Fax 301.718.2243
Email Shemro@aol.com

Client
Shemro Engineering
Design Firm
Blank—Robert Kent Wilson
Designer
Robert Kent Wilson

PARC METROPOLITAN

133 METROPOLITAN DRIVE MILPITAS, CA 95035 TEL 408.934.5800 FAX 408.934.1850

Client
RGC Developers
Design Firm
Visual Asylum
Designers
Joel Sotelo, Amy Jo Levine, MaeLin Levine

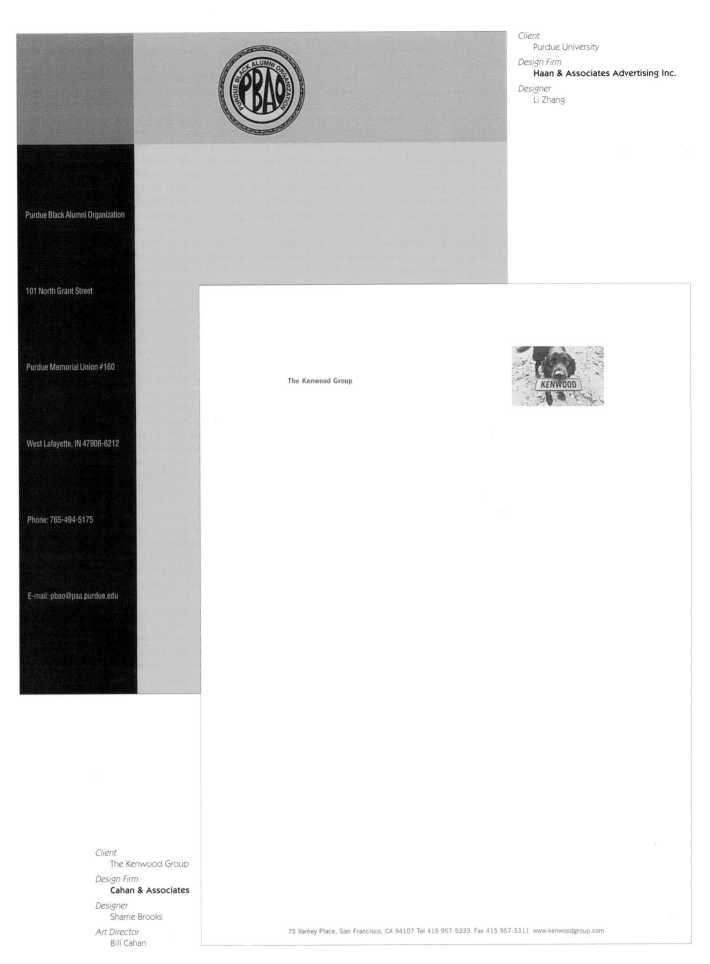

Client
  Purdue University
Design Firm
  Haan & Associates Advertising Inc.
Designer
  Li Zhang

Purdue Black Alumni Organization

101 North Grant Street

Purdue Memorial Union #160

West Lafayette, IN 47906-6212

Phone: 765-494-5175

E-mail: pbao@paa.purdue.edu

The Kenwood Group

KENWOOD

Client
  The Kenwood Group
Design Firm
  Cahan & Associates
Designer
  Sharrie Brooks
Art Director
  Bill Cahan

75 Varney Place, San Francisco, CA 94107 Tel 415 957-5333 Fax 415 957-5311 www.kenwoodgroup.com

STROKE PREVENTION SPEAKERS CONFERENCE

Client
Boehringer Ingelheim
Pharmaceuticals, Inc.

Design Firm
**Health Science
Communications, Inc.**

Designer
Robert Padovano

METROPOLITAN

BALLROOM & CLUBROOM

Client
D'Amico & Partners

Design Firm
Little & Company

Designer
Tom Riddle

Design Director
Jim Jackson

5418 Wayzata Boulevard Minneapolis, Minnesota 55416 T 612 797 1900 F 612 797 1910

153

redhat

Red Hat Software, Inc.
3203 Yorktown Avenue Suite 123 Durham, NC 27713
919.572.6500 FAX 919.572.6726 www.redhat.com

Client
 Red Hat Software
Design Firm
 Blank—Robert Kent Wilson
Designers
 Robert Kent Wilson,
 Suzanne Ultman, Adam Cohn

incube8.com

www.incube8.com 2400 Boston St., The Signature Building 3rd Floor Baltimore, MD 21224 tel: 410.732.7300 fax: 410.685.2616

Client
 Incube8.com
Design Firm
 Gr8
Art Director
 Lisa Wurfl-Roeca
Designer
 Alain Bolduc

Client
Badlanders

Design Firm
Girvin

Designer
Kevin Henderson

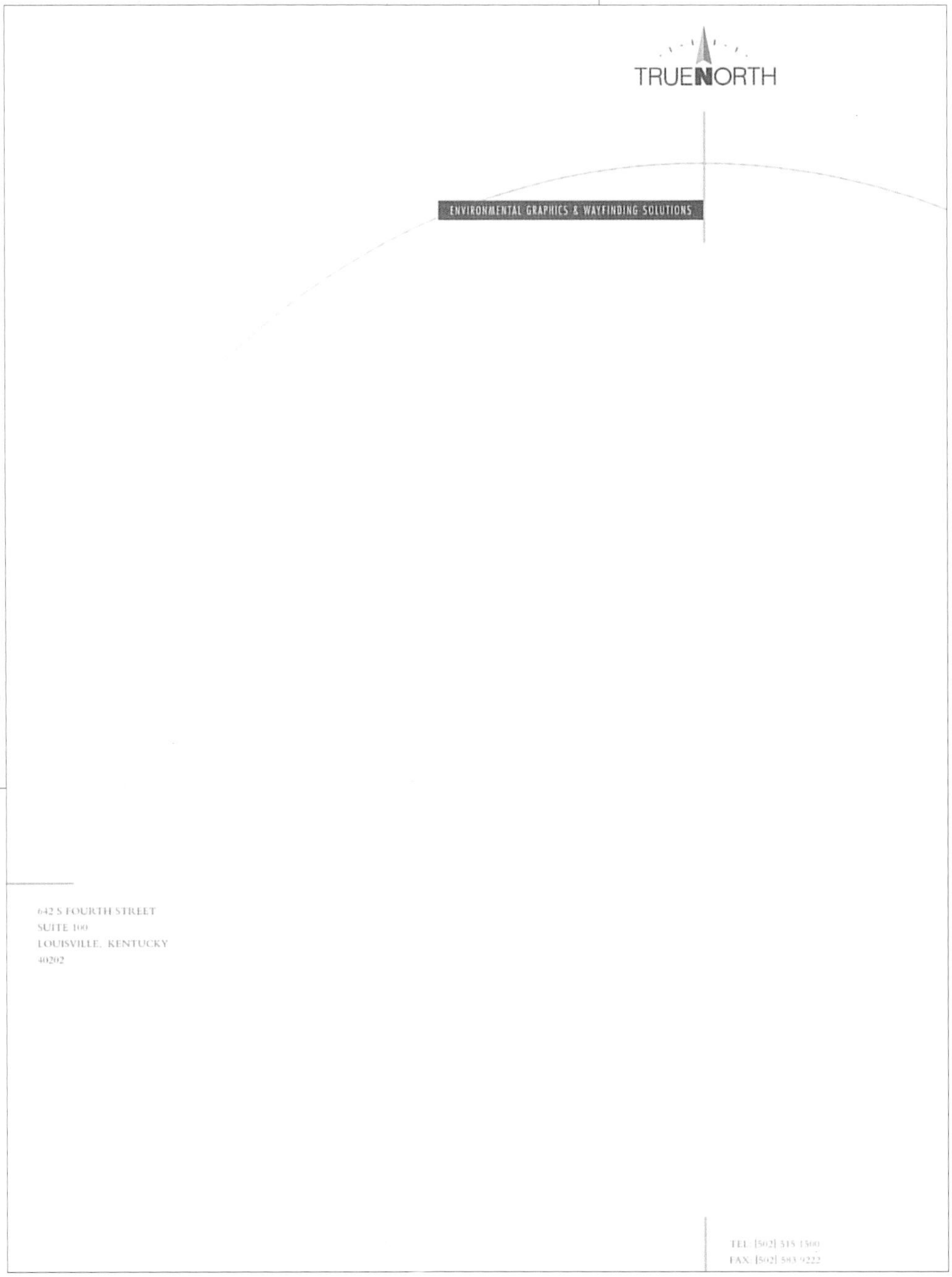

TRUENORTH

ENVIRONMENTAL GRAPHICS & WAYFINDING SOLUTIONS

642 S FOURTH STREET
SUITE 100
LOUISVILLE, KENTUCKY
40202

TEL [502] 515-1300
FAX [502] 583-5222

Client
True North

Design Firm
Abney/Huninghake Design Group

Designer
Cheryl Smith

j.p. & associates *meeting planning & consulting*

914 Mercer Boulevard

Suite 4

Omaha, NE 68131

juliepierce@uswest.net

tel 402.556.6645

fax 402.556.6645

Client
Julie Pierce & Associates

Design Firm
Webster Design Associates

Designers
Sean Heisler, Dave Webster

SHAMAN
Good Medicine For Technology

2415 Third St.
Suite 231
San Francisco,
CA 94107

www.eShaman.com

Client
Shaman

Design Firm
Diesel Design

Designer
Amy Bainbridge

Space Needle
The View

Live the View

203 6th Avenue North
Seattle, WA 98109-5005
Main: (206) 443-9700
Fax: (206) 441-7415

Client
  Space Needle
Design Firm
  Hornall Anderson Design Works
Designers
  Jack Anderson,
  Mary Hermes, Gretchen Cook,
  Andrew Smith, Julie Lock

Counterpane
Internet Security, Inc.

3031 Tisch Way, 100 Plaza East · San Jose, California 95128 · USA
408-260-7500 · Fax 408-556-0889 · http://www.counterpane.com

Client
  Counterpane
Design Firm
  Tollner Design Group
Designer
  Terry Wetmore

crescent systems
a software consulting group

crescent systems, LLC
suite 504
3 bethesda metro center
bethesda, MD 20814
phone: 301.657.8277
fax: 301.657.8201
url: www.crescent.cc

Client
Crescent Systems

Design Firm
Tim Kenney Design Partners

Creative Director
Tim Kenney

Designer
Jamie Stockie

RK WITT and Associates, Inc.

A
suite 345
merchandise mart plaza
chicago illinois 60654
T
312 329 WITT
F
312 329 1037

REPRESENTING A COMPLETE LINE OF
COMMERCIAL & OFFICE FURNISHINGS

Client
RK Witt and Associates, Inc.

Design Firm
Rauscher Design Inc.

Designers
Christian Paeth,
Russ Jackson, Janet Rauscher

Client
  Kimpton Hotel & Restaurant Group
Design Firm
  Hunt Weber Clark Assoc., Inc.
Designers
  Leigh Krichbaum, Nancy Hunt-Weber

SERRANO HOTEL
SAN FRANCISCO

international golf discount

2340 towne lake parkway, suite 120 | woodstock, georgia 30189
phone 770 517 2280 | fax 770 517 2854 | toll free 877 99G BALL

405 TAYLOR STREET
SAN FRANCISCO CA 94102
TELEPHONE 415.885.2500
FACSIMILE 415.474.4879
RESERVATIONS 877.294.9709
WWW.SERRANOHOTEL.COM

gball.com

Client
  Gball.com
Design Firm
  Mires Design
Designer
  Miguel Perez
Illustrator
  Tracy Sabin

Client
   Matthew Borkoski Photography

Design Firm
   Tim Kenney Design Partners

Creative Director
   Tim Kenney

Designer
   John Bowen

>ADDRESS   191 East Broad Street
>   Suite 319
>   Athens, GA 30601
>   >>
>PHONE *   706-353-9530
>   >>
>FAX *   706-353-6230
>   >>>
>WEB SITE   www.radar-mp.com

Client
   Radar Multimedia Productions, Inc.

Design Firm
   Diesel Design

Designer
   Will Yarbrough

WISE*Place*

A community of housing and hope

for women inspir

Client
  WISE Place
Design Firm
  Engle + Murphy
Designer
  Emily Moe

NES·KNOWLTON

Architects

Nancy Nes
David Knowlton

Email nesknow@aol.com
Phone 410.625.0316   Fax 410.625.1714
413 East Hamburg Street Baltimore, Maryland 21230

1411 North Broadway, Santa Ana, CA 92706 *p*

Client
  Nes Knowlton Architects
Design Firm
  Blank—Robert Kent Wilson
Designers
  Robert Kent Wilson, Suzanne Ultman

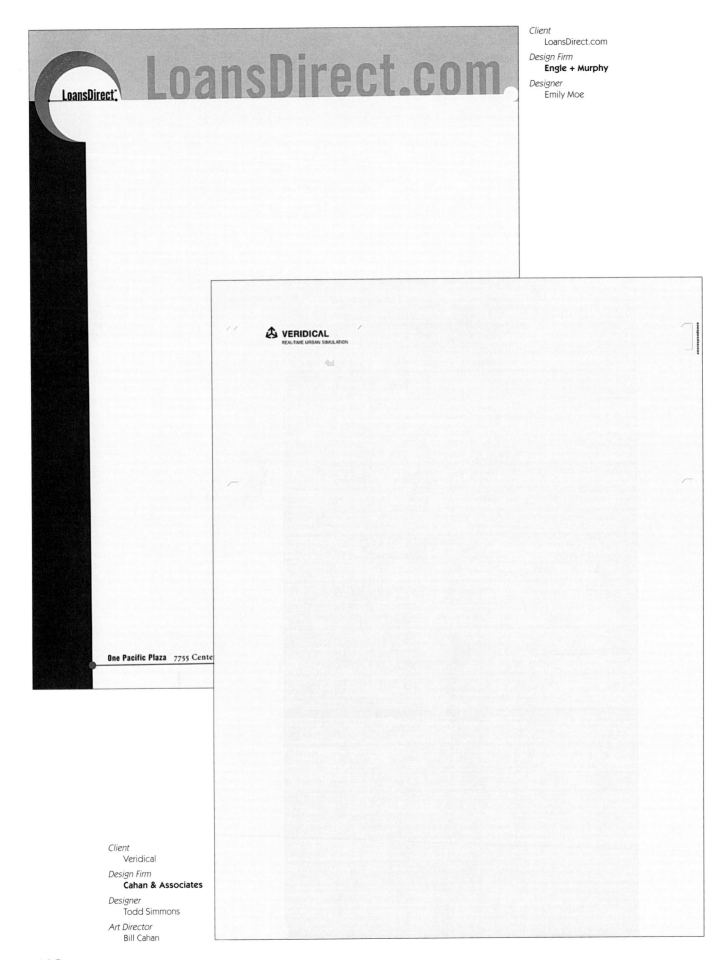

Client
LoansDirect.com

Design Firm
Engle + Murphy

Designer
Emily Moe

LoansDirect.com

LoansDirect™

VERIDICAL
REAL-TIME URBAN SIMULATION

One Pacific Plaza 7755 Center

Client
Veridical

Design Firm
Cahan & Associates

Designer
Todd Simmons

Art Director
Bill Cahan

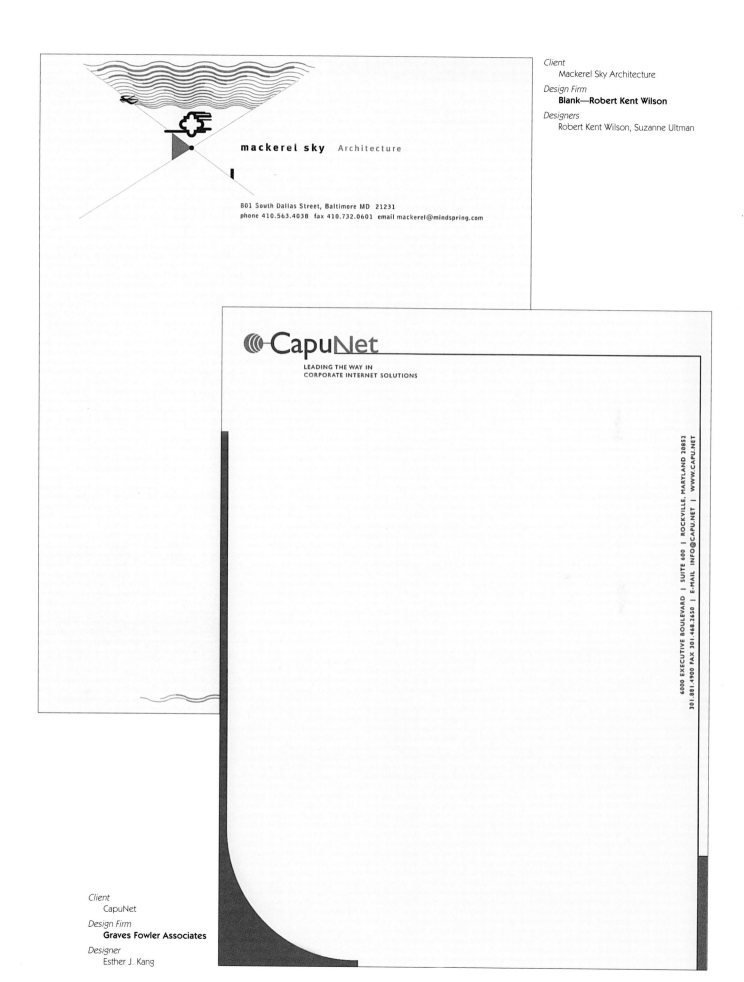

mackerel sky Architecture

801 South Dallas Street, Baltimore MD 21231
phone 410.563.4038 fax 410.732.0601 email mackerel@mindspring.com

Client
Mackerel Sky Architecture
Design Firm
Blank—Robert Kent Wilson
Designers
Robert Kent Wilson, Suzanne Ultman

CapuNet

LEADING THE WAY IN
CORPORATE INTERNET SOLUTIONS

6000 EXECUTIVE BOULEVARD | SUITE 600 | ROCKVILLE, MARYLAND 20852
301.881.4900 FAX 301.468.2650 | E-MAIL INFO@CAPU.NET | WWW.CAPU.NET

Client
CapuNet
Design Firm
Graves Fowler Associates
Designer
Esther J. Kang

163

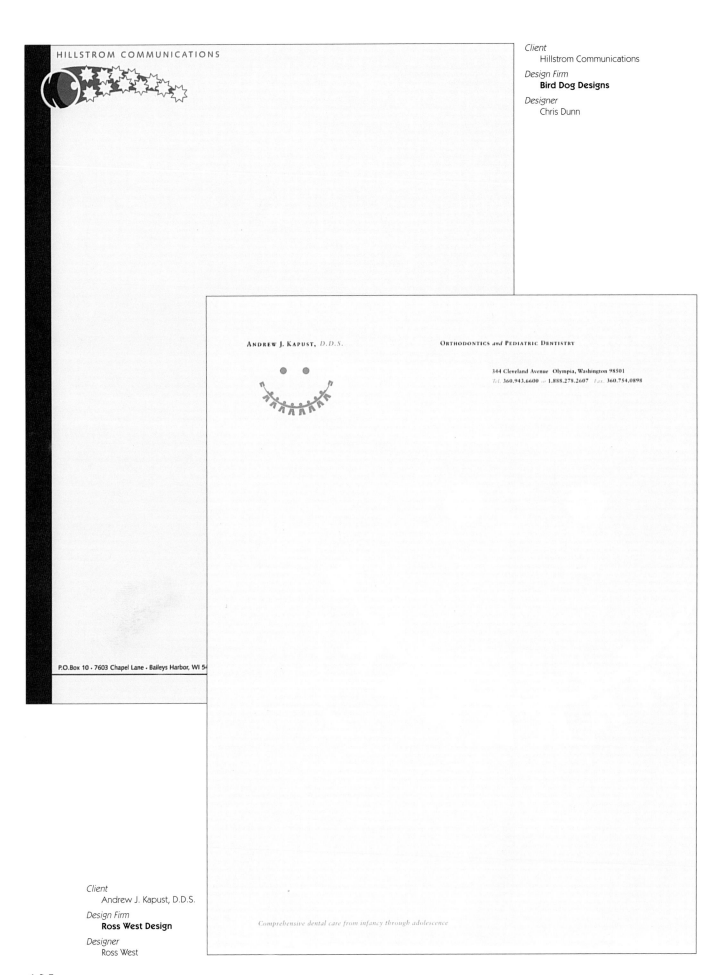

HILLSTROM COMMUNICATIONS

P.O.Box 10 · 7603 Chapel Lane · Baileys Harbor, WI 54

ANDREW J. KAPUST, D.D.S.

ORTHODONTICS and PEDIATRIC DENTISTRY

344 Cleveland Avenue Olympia, Washington 98501
Tel. 360.943.6600 or 1.888.278.2607 Fax 360.754.0898

Comprehensive dental care from infancy through adolescence

Client
Hillstrom Communications

Design Firm
Bird Dog Designs

Designer
Chris Dunn

Client
Andrew J. Kapust, D.D.S.

Design Firm
Ross West Design

Designer
Ross West

Client
    Studioluscious
Design Firm
    Studioluscious
Designers
    Susan Hessler, Jennifer Fredritz, Gilberto Albuquerque

tel 614.442.6775
fax 614.442.6831

albudes8@earthlink.net

VERIDA

Verida Internet Corp. 50 California Street, Suite 1500, San Francisco, CA 94111
Toll Free: 1-877-VERIDA1 Phone: 415.464.8600 Fax: 415.464.8660 www.verida.com

Client
    Verida Internet Corp.
Design Firm
    Triad, Inc.
Designers
    Diana Kollanyi, Michael Hinshaw

165

goinet

go**i**net

www.goinet.com

210 N. Tucker Blvd.

Suite 240

St. Louis, MO 63101

phone: (314) 504-4300

fax (314) 212-5177

Client
goinet
Design Firm
Stan Gellman Graphic Design Inc.
Designers
Erin Goter, Barry Tilson

telephone
760 . 438 . 7488

facsimile
760 . 438 . 2560

randall
I N T E R N A T I O N A L
2885 Loker Avenue East
Carlsbad, California 92008-6626

villa

R A N D A L L I N T E R N A T I O N A L . C O M

Client
Randall International
Design Firm
Randall International
Designer
Randall International
In-House Design Team

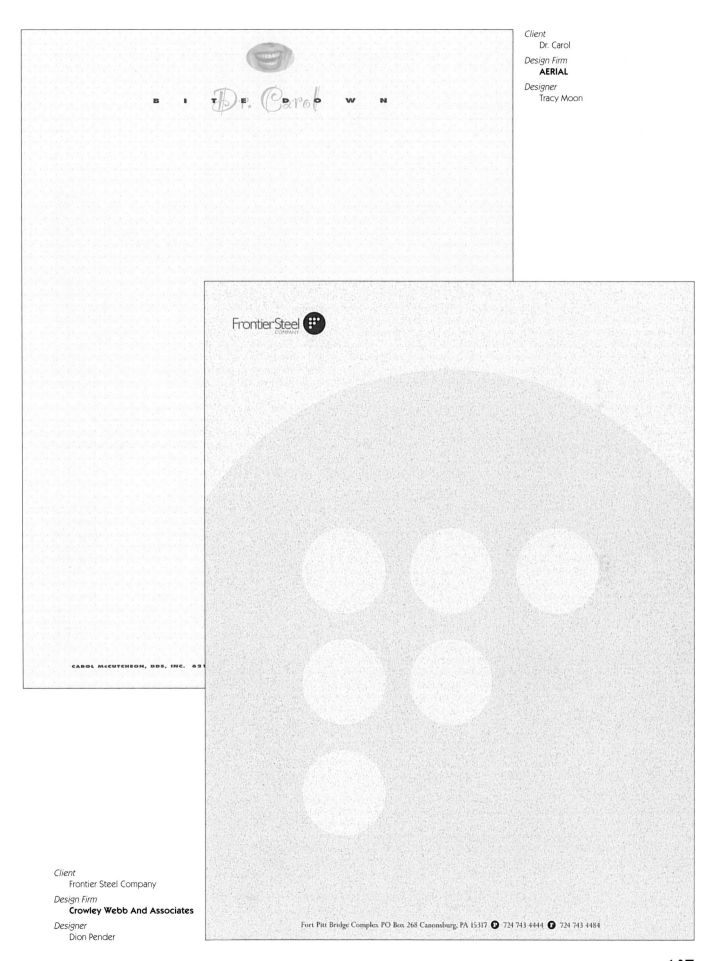

Client
    Dr. Carol
Design Firm
    AERIAL
Designer
    Tracy Moon

BITE DOWN

Dr. Carol

CAROL McCUTCHEON, DDS, INC. 621

FrontierSteel
COMPANY

Fort Pitt Bridge Complex PO Box 268 Canonsburg, PA 15317 **P** 724 743 4444 **F** 724 743 4484

Client
    Frontier Steel Company
Design Firm
    Crowley Webb And Associates
Designer
    Dion Pender

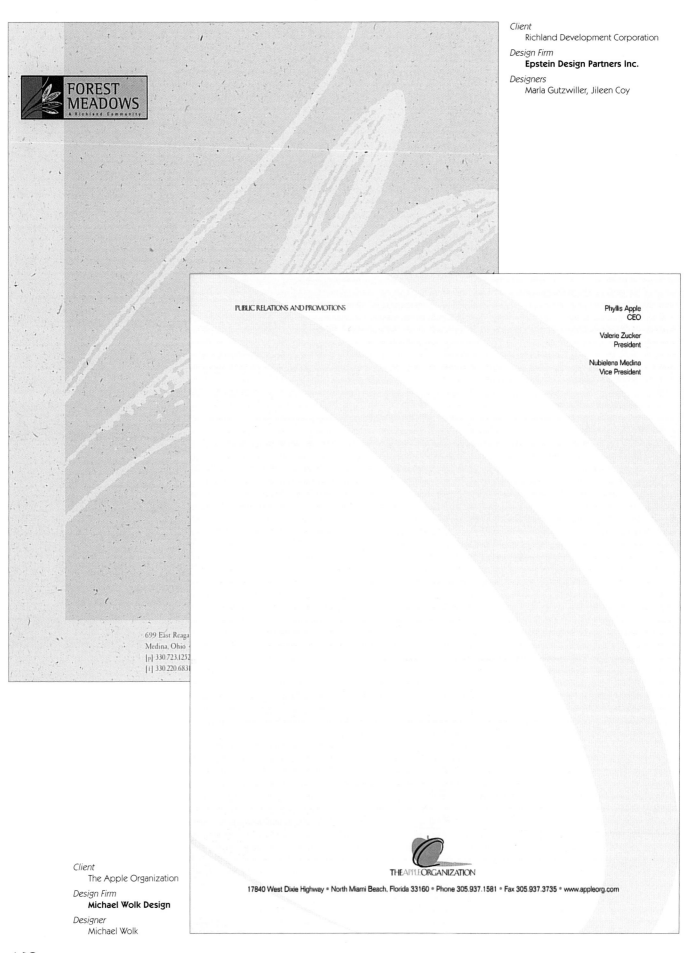

Client
Richland Development Corporation

Design Firm
Epstein Design Partners Inc.

Designers
Marla Gutzwiller, Jileen Coy

FOREST
MEADOWS
A Richland Community

699 East Reaga
Medina, Ohio
[p] 330.723.1252
[t] 330.220.6831

PUBLIC RELATIONS AND PROMOTIONS

Phyllis Apple
CEO

Valerie Zucker
President

Nubielena Medina
Vice President

THE APPLE ORGANIZATION

17840 West Dixie Highway ▪ North Miami Beach, Florida 33160 ▪ Phone 305.937.1581 ▪ Fax 305.937.3735 ▪ www.appleorg.com

Client
The Apple Organization

Design Firm
Michael Wolk Design

Designer
Michael Wolk

Client
  Flourish
Design Firm
  Flourish
Designers
  Christopher Ferranti,
  Jing Lauengco, Henry Frey

flourish™

BRADLEY BUILDING | 1220 W 6TH S

6000 S. Eastern Avenue Suite 10A Las Vegas NV 89119 Phone 702 739 0246 Fax 702 736 0901

kill the messenger

Client
  kill the messenger
Design Firm
  Crowley Webb and Associates
Designer
  Brian Grunert

4151 N. Humboldt Avenue
Milwaukee, WI 53212-9979

Phone 414 961 0310
Fax 414 961 1070

Client
   Wisconsin Humane Society

Design Firm
   H2D

Creative Specialist
   Jennifer Peck

Art Director
   Joseph Hausch

P.
316.262.6733

F.
316·262·1167

Paul Chauncey
PHOTOGRAPHIC
EXCELLENCE

388 N. HYDRAULIC
WICHITA, KANSAS 67214

E-MAIL: CHAUNCEYPC@AOL.COM   WWW.CHAUNCEYPHOTO.COM

Client
   Paul Chauncey Photography

Design Firm
   Gardner Design

Designers
   Brian Miller, Bill Gardner

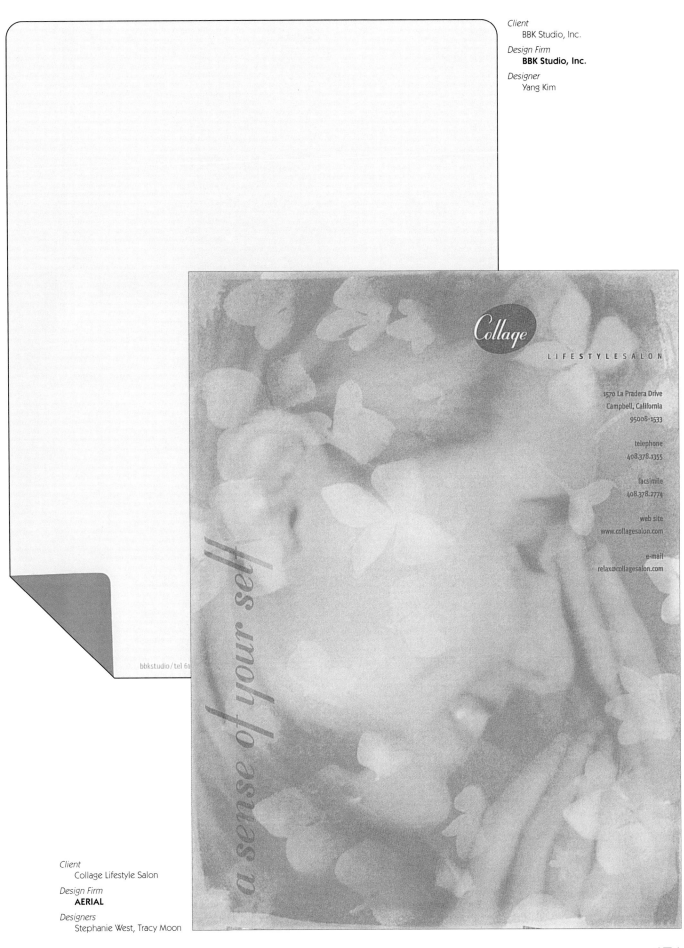

Client
    BBK Studio, Inc.
Design Firm
    BBK Studio, Inc.
Designer
    Yang Kim

a sense of your self

Collage
LIFESTYLESALON

1570 La Pradera Drive
Campbell, California
95008-1533

telephone
408.378.1355

facsimile
408.378.2774

web site
www.collagesalon.com

e-mail
relax@collagesalon.com

bbkstudio/tel 61

Client
    Collage Lifestyle Salon
Design Firm
    AERIAL
Designers
    Stephanie West, Tracy Moon

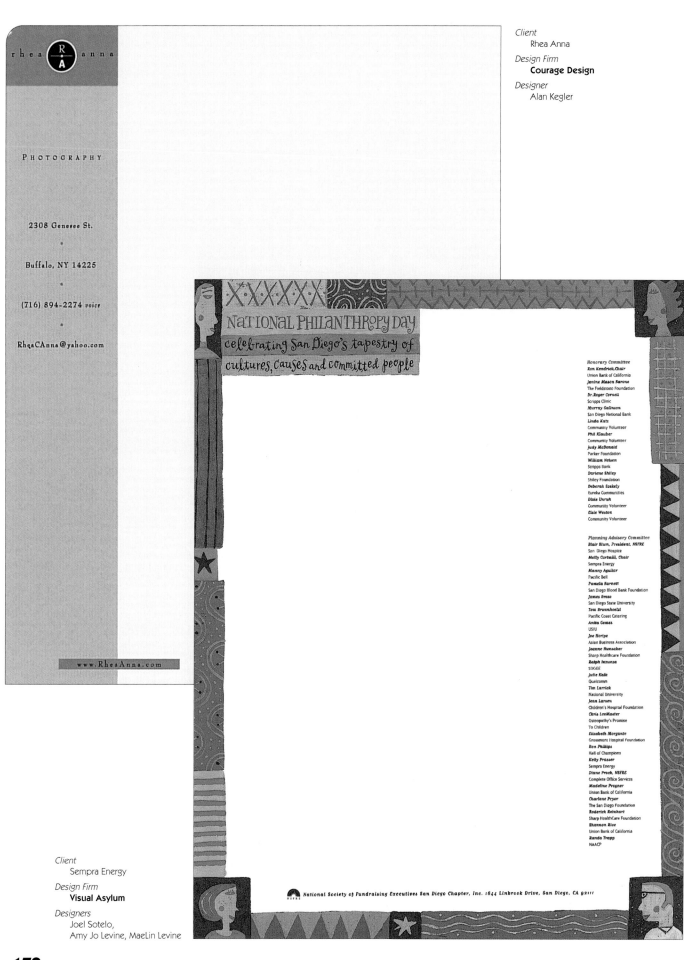

rhea R|A anna

PHOTOGRAPHY

2308 Genesee St.

·

Buffalo, NY 14225

·

(716) 894-2274 voice

·

RheaCAnna@yahoo.com

www.RheaAnna.com

Client
Rhea Anna
Design Firm
Courage Design
Designer
Alan Kegler

NATIONAL PHILANTHROPY DAY
celebrating San Diego's tapestry of
cultures, causes and committed people

Honorary Committee
Ron Kendrick, Chair
Union Bank of California
Janine Mason Barone
The Fieldstone Foundation
Dr. Roger Cornell
Scripps Clinic
Murray Galinson
San Diego National Bank
Linda Katz
Community Volunteer
Phil Klauber
Community Volunteer
Judy McDonald
Parker Foundation
William Nelsen
Scripps Bank
Darlene Shiley
Shiley Foundation
Deborah Szekely
Eureka Communities
Dixie Unruh
Community Volunteer
Elsie Weston
Community Volunteer

Planning Advisory Committee
Blair Blum, President, NSFRE
San Diego Hospice
Molly Cartmill, Chair
Sempra Energy
Manny Aguilar
Pacific Bell
Pamela Barnett
San Diego Blood Bank Foundation
James Brose
San Diego State University
Tom Brunnhoelzl
Pacific Coast Catering
Anita Gomes
USIU
Joe Horiye
Asian Business Association
Jeanne Hunsaker
Sharp Healthcare Foundation
Ralph Inzunza
SDG&E
Julie Kalk
Qualcomm
Tim Larrick
National University
Jenn Larsen
Children's Hospital Foundation
Chris LeeMaster
Osteopathy's Promise
To Children
Elizabeth Morgante
Grossmont Hospital Foundation
Ron Phillips
Hall of Champions
Kelly Prosser
Sempra Energy
Diane Prock, NSFRE
Complete Office Services
Madeline Progner
Union Bank of California
Charlene Pryor
The San Diego Foundation
Roderick Reinhart
Sharp HealthCare Foundation
Shannon Rice
Union Bank of California
Randa Trapp
NAACP

National Society of Fundraising Executives San Diego Chapter, Inc. 1644 Linbrook Drive, San Diego, CA 92111

Client
Sempra Energy
Design Firm
Visual Asylum
Designers
Joel Sotelo,
Amy Jo Levine, MaeLin Levine

172

Client
    imind Corporation
Design Firm
    Hornall Anderson Design Works
Designers
    Jack Anderson, Debra McCloskey,
    Anne Johnston, Tobi Brown,
    Henry Yiu, John Anderle

(m)nd™

JEFFERSON
AT MILL CREEK
AN ESTATES APARTMENT COMMUNITY

14420 NORTH CREEK DRIVE
MILL CREEK, WA 98012
TEL 425.379.7799
FAX 425.379.7878
WWW.JPI.COM

Client
    Jefferson Properties, Inc.
Design Firm
    VWA Group, Inc.
Designer
    Brian Blankenship

Client
  Meredith & Crew
Design Firm
  Belyea
Designers
  Patricia Belyea, Naomi Murphy

Meredith
& crew

4675 MacArthur Court Ste. 1150
Newport Beach, CA 92660
Phone 949.724.4833
Fax 949.724.4839

winfire™

Client
  Winfire
Design Firm
  Evenson Design Group
Designers
  Mark Sojka, Karen Barranco

the shadowlight group

150 North Queen Street
Studio Suite 200
Lancaster, PA 17603

717 396 4132 phone
717 396 4458 fax
shadowlightgroup.com

85 EXCHANGE STREET PORTLAND ME 04101

207 775 5100 F 207 775 5147 www.owgroup.com

Client
  the shadowlight group
Design Firm
  Albert/Bogner
  Design Communications
Designers
  Ed Zuschmidt, Kelly Albert

Client
  DW Group
Design Firm
  DW Group
Designer
  Kyle C. Murphy

Client
    Uncommon Grounds
Design Firm
    Kowalski Designworks Inc.
Designers
    Carrie Wallahan, Derrick Wynes

14131 Midway Road • Suite 500 • Addison, Texas 75001 • Tel: 972-801-8800 • Fax: 972-943-6030 • www.vast.com

Client
    Vast Solutions
Design Firm
    Addison Whitney
Designer
    Kimberlee Davis

B.J. Armstrong Custom Homes

POST OFFICE BOX 633 · BLOO

Client
   B.J. Armstrong Custom Homes
Design Firm
   Julie Johnson Design
Designer
   Julie Johnson

Suite 540 · Ford Center
420 N. Fifth Street
Minneapolis, MN 55401
3 LEGGED RACE
NEW THEATER &
PERFORMANCE
Ph. No (612) 332-3200
Fax No (612) 332-3207

race

Client
   3 Legged Race
Design Firm
   Pat Carney Studio, Inc.
Designer
   Millie Hanson

177

Client
Atlantis Restaurant

Design Firm
pollen 8 studios

Designer
Cory Sheehan

ATLANTIS
R E S T A U R A N T

1880 Harbor Island Drive
San Diego, CA 92101
(P) 619 / 297 / 1073
(F) 619 / 297 / 9125

PROFESSIONAL
TITLE SERVICING

Vox 818.551.9258

Client
Professional Title Service

Design Firm
Egad Dzyn

Designer
Steve Trapero

Client
Hekimian

Design Firm
Addison Whitney

Designer
Logan Watts

15200 Omega Drive · Rockville, MD 20850

ph 301.590.3600

www.hekimian.com

Hekimian
A AN AXEL JOHNSON INC. COMPANY

karen dean©
THE OUT TO LUNCH GAL

12 Hawthorne Hill

Louisville, KY 40204

502-459-7876

Cookin' up music and dishin' out fun!

Client
Karen Dean

Design Firm
Abney/Huninghake Design Group

Designer
Karen Abney

Client
  Casa Bonita
Design Firm
  Sayles Graphic Design
Designer
  John Sayles

431 HIGHWAY 179 / SEDONA,

5205 grant avenue, cleveland, ohio 44125
216 641-7148   216 641-7147   info@readyeddiego.com

readyeddiego.**com**.

Client
  internet eddie company
Design Firm
  Design Room
Designers
  Chad Gordon, Kevin Rathge

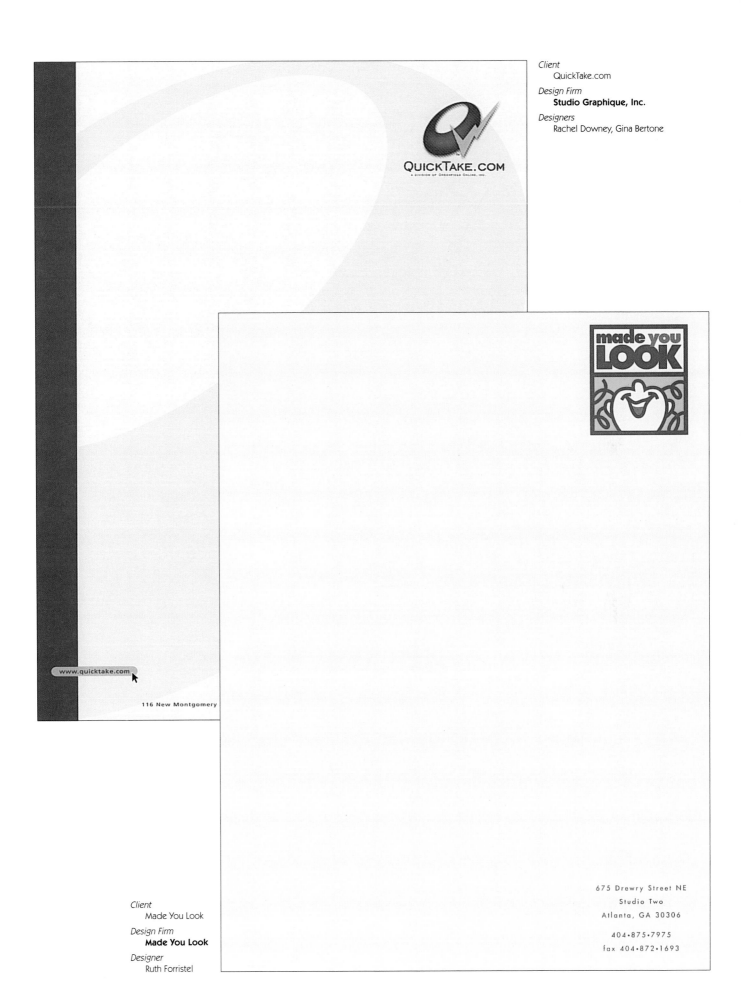

Client
  QuickTake.com
Design Firm
  Studio Graphique, Inc.
Designers
  Rachel Downey, Gina Bertone

QUICKTAKE.COM
A DIVISION OF GREENFIELD ONLINE, INC.

www.quicktake.com

116 New Montgomery

made you
LOOK

675 Drewry Street NE
Studio Two
Atlanta, GA 30306

404•875•7975
fax 404•872•1693

Client
  Made You Look
Design Firm
  Made You Look
Designer
  Ruth Forristel

Client
    Dalton Design Inc.
Design Firm
    Dalton Design Inc.
Designer
    Annmarie Dalton

3101 N. Tenaya Way • Las Vegas, NV 89128   Ph: (702) 36-CREEK (362-7335),• Fax (702) 362-7336

Client
    Tenaya Creek Restaurant & Brewery
Design Firm
    Creative Dynamics
Designers
    Dawn Teagarden,
    Victor Rodriguez, Casey Corcoran

Client
  Jet-Golf
Design Firm
  LKF Marketing
Designer
  Sue Severeid

www • jet-golf • com

303 North Rose Street • Suite 410 • Kal

EDUCATION
to go

P.O. Box 760, Temecula, California 92593-0760 ■ voice 800.701.8755 ■ fax 909.506.6547

Client
  Education to Go
Design Firm
  Winter Graphic South
Designer
  Mary Winter

Client
  IMLOGO
Design Firm
  Imtech Communications
Designer
  Robert Keng

Client
  EMS technologies, inc.
Design Firm
  Studio Graphique, Inc.
Designers
  Rachel Downey,
  Gina Bertone, William G. Marconi Jr.

184

Client
  Bird Design
Design Firm
  Bird Design
Creative Director
  Peter King Robbins

CLEARDATA.NET

5956 Sherry Lane Dallas, TX 75225 phone 214.750.1599 fax 214.750.7086

Client
  ClearData.net
Design Firm
  After Hours Creative
Designer
  After Hours Creative

WatchGuard®
TECHNOLOGIES, INC.

316 Occidental Ave. S., Suite 200
Seattle, WA 98104

T 206.521.8340
F 206.521.8342
www.watchguard.com

Client
WatchGuard Technologies, Inc.
Design Firm
Hornall Anderson Design Works
Designers
Jack Anderson,
Lisa Cerveny, Mary Hermes,
Kathy Saito, Michael Brugman,
Holly Craven, Belinda Bowling

Client
IWin.com
Design Firm
Bird Design
Creative Director
Peter King Robbins
Art Director
Etienne Jardel

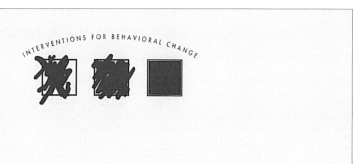

Client
  Interventions for Behavioral Change
Design Firm
  Steve Morris
Designer
  Steve Morris

Xyvision Enterprise Solutions, Inc.
30 New Crossing Road Reading, MA 01867-3254

XyEnterprise

P.O. BOX 1206 •

tel: 781.756.4400   fax: 781.756.4300   www.xyenterprise.com

Client
  Xyvision Enterprise Solutions, Inc.
Design Firm
  Stewart Monderer Design, Inc.
Designers
  Joseph La Roche, Stewart Monderer

Client
    Crescent Networks
Design Firm
    Stewart Monderer Design, Inc.
Designer
    Aime Lecusay

CRESCENT
networks

www.crescentnets.com

201 riverneck road   chelmsford, ma 01824

t 978 244 9002   f 978 244 9211

30sixty design, inc
2801 cahuenga boulevard west
los angeles ca 90068
ph 323 850 5311
        fax 323 850 6638

www.30sixtydesign.com

Client
    30sixty design, inc.
Design Firm
    30sixty design, inc.
Designers
    Henry Vizcarra, Anna Kalinka

distilled images
a picture's worth

eighty-five bluxome
san francisco californ
t 415.618.0530 f 415.618
www.distilledimages

Client
    Distilled Images
Design Firm
    AERIAL
Designers
    Tracy Moon, Misty Bralver

da Vinci
DA VINCI BY DESIGN

832 Fifth Avenue, Suite 12   San Diego, CA 92101   t 619 238 0207   f 619 238 1229   www.davincibydesign.com

Client
    da Vinci By Design
Design Firm
    Buchanan Design
Designer
    Bobby Buchanan

Client
  Wild Hare
Design Firm
  Anvil Graphic Design
Designer
  Gary Wong

WILD HARE

1029 El Camino Real   Menlo Park, California 94025

tel 650.327.HARE (4273)   fax 650.327.4276

LEOPARD

www.leopard.com

303.527.2900

6230 lookout road
boulder, co 80301

303.530.3480

Client
  Leopard
Design Firm
  Leopard
Designers
  Brendan Hemp,
  Andy Rahl, Nita Herupermatasari

GartzkePhoto**graphy**

117 West Walker, Studio 301
Milwaukee, WI 53201

Phone 414.643.8181
Fax 414.643.7828

E-mail algartzke@bubblers.com

Location
Studio
Digital

Client
  Gartzke Photography
Design Firm
  H2D
Art Director
  Joseph Hausch

ℰ

EuroArte
1360 REGENT STREET, SUITE 192
MADISON, WISCONSIN 53715
PHONE 800.351.7723
FAX 608.245.9743

Client
  Euroarte
Design Firm
  Planet Design
Designer
  Brad DeMarea

Camacho Commercial | Real Estate Services

CAMACHO
COMMERCIAL

LOS ANGELES 660 S. Figueroa Street
Suite 700
Los Angeles, CA 90017

PASADENA 1540 N. Lake Avenue
Pasadena, CA 91104

626/791-8005 PHONE
626/791-7123 FAX

INTERNET www.camacho.net

Client
Camacho Commercial
Design Firm
FOCUS
Design and Marketing Solutions
Designer
Aram Youssefian

200 Brown Road #208 Fremont CA 94539 (510) 623-0472 (510) 438-0839 fax

Client
La Freniere & Associates
Design Firm
Brad Terres Design
Designer
Brad Terres

CORPORATE ID MANUALS

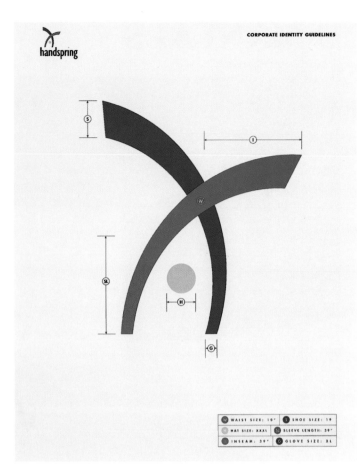

Client
    Handspring, Inc.
Design Firm
    Mortensen Design
Art Director
    Gordon Mortensen
Designers
    Gordon Mortensen, PJ Nidecker

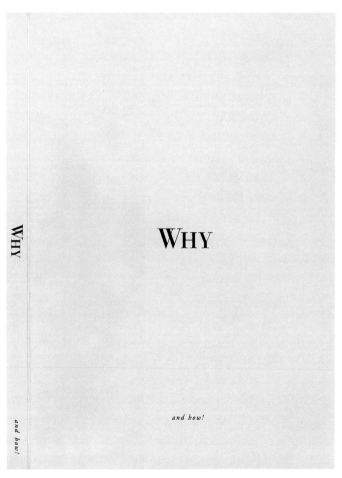

Client
    Steelcase, Inc.
Design Firm
    Genesis, Inc.
Designers
    Jim Adler, Beth Kreimer

Client
   Guidance Inc.
Design Firm
   Baker Designed Communications
Designers
   Brian Keenen, Gary Baker

fig 2.2 Acceptable Colors

fig 2.3 Unacceptable Colors

graphic style guide →

🔄 **guidance**

Acceptable Color Applications

The colors for the Corporate Signature are Guidance Blue and Guidance Green. Guidance Yellow has been chosen as a third color to use as an accent color for design applications. (See fig. 2.1.)

When only one color is specified, you should always use Guidance Blue or Black. Use a 50 percent screen to simulate the second color except when overlaying a photo. In this case, 100% white or black is recommended. (See fig. 2.2.)

When design dictates, you may want to reverse the Corporate Signature. Be sure to choose background colors that offer sufficient contrast (i.e., Guidance Blue or black).

Note: Additional colors that can be used in corporate communications are black and white. Any variations from this color palette must be approved by the Marketing Group.

Unacceptable Color Applications

The corporate colors were carefully selected. It is therefore imperative that we never vary from the approved color applications. Please, never transpose or alter the assigned colors of the elements in any way. (See fig. 2.3.)

Client
   Consumers Interstate Corporation
Design Firm
   O & J Design Inc.
Art Director
   Andrzej Olejniczak
Designer
   Lia Camara-Mariscal

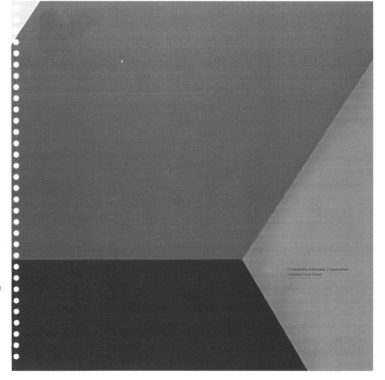

⁄h Bank of Hawaii

Signature
Logotype
Symbol
Subsidiaries
Color
Typography
Branding
Stationery
Forms

Corporate
Identity System
Manual

Client
Pacific Century Financial Corp.
Design Firm
Eric Woo Design Inc.
Designers
Eric Woo, Steven Tabusi

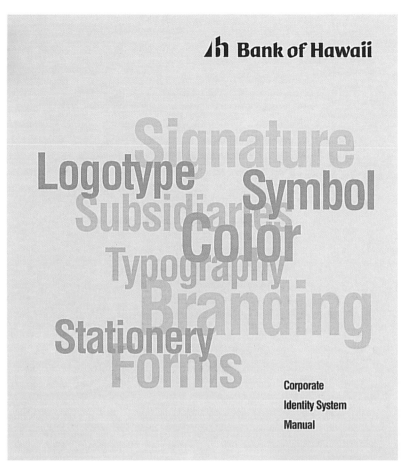

Client
Praxair, Inc.
Design Firm
ilardi design
Designers
Salvatore Ilardi, Jason Nocera

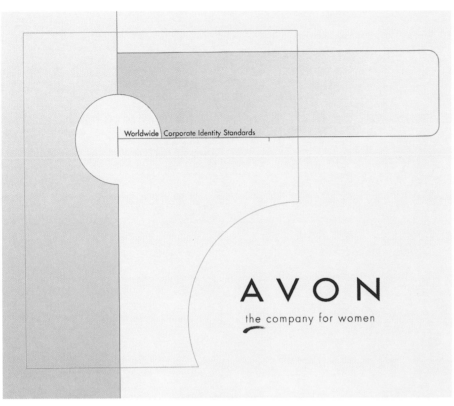

Client
  Avon Products, Inc.
Design Firm
  O & J Design, Inc.
Art Director
  Andrzej Olejniczak
Designers
  Lia Camara-Mariscal,
  Christina Mueller, Sasha Swetschinski

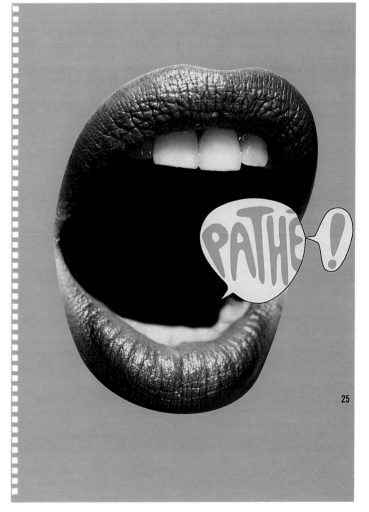

Client
  Pathé
Design Firm
  Landor Associates
Designers
  Margaret Youngblood, Eric Scott,
  Doug Sellers, Kirsten Tarnowski, Michele Berry

197

KODAK *Identity Guidelines*

TAKE PICTURES. FURTHER.™

Corporate Identity Guidelines

sgi

Client
Eastman Kodak Company

Design Firm
Forward

Designers
Duke Stofer, Julie Forward, Karen Kress

Client
SGI

Design Firm
Landor Associates

Designers
Patrick Cox, Frank Mueller

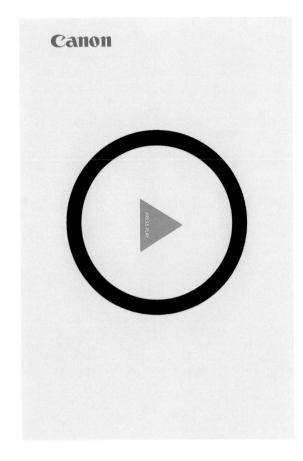

PRESS PLAY

Client
  Canon

Design Firm
  Interbrand

Designers
  Interbrand Design Team

Yes! You have reached the end... but it really is just the beginning...

Stacked, Flush Left Version

3Com®
More connected.™

Preferred format for most applications,
including collateral and packaging.

Single Line Version

3Com® More connected.™

Second preferred format. Effective in wide horizontal
applications, such as double spread display ads.

Stacked, Flush Right Version

3Com®
More connected.™

Format for right alignment
situations only.

Example of brochure back cover using the
stacked flush left version.

Advertisement example using the single line version.

56K Fax Modem
#1 selling modem in the world!

Product flyer example using the stacked flush
right version.

Client
  3 Com

Design Firm
  Sapient

Designers
  Patsy Hayer, Michael Conti

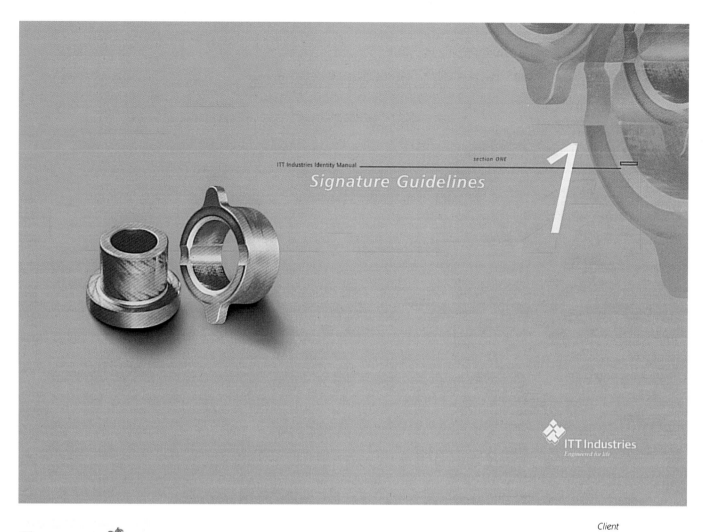

ITT Industries Identity Manual .... section ONE

Signature Guidelines

1

ITT Industries
Engineered for life

Signature Guidelines

The ITT Industries signature is a graphic expression of our new identity. It is bold, solid and distinctive, evoking an image of strength, deliberateness and carefully "engineered" precision. These guidelines have been prepared with the same thorough exactness.

The signature's combined elements—symbol, logotype and tagline—clearly establish our mission as engineers. Our tagline, "Engineered for life," reinforces the essence of who we are. Our ability to communicate effectively in all the environments where our identity lives requires a family of signature variations. When properly selected, the right signature for the right environment will provide equally strong communication to its viewer.

Client
ITT

Design Firm
Landor Associates

Designer
Jamie Calderon

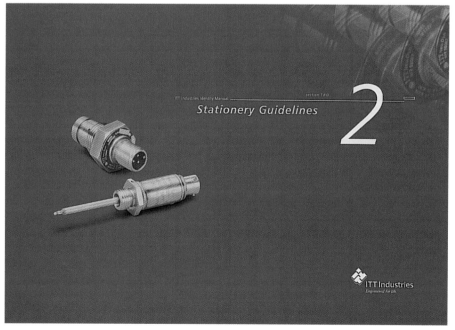

ITT Industries Identity Manual .... section TWO

Stationery Guidelines

2

ITT Industries
Engineered for life

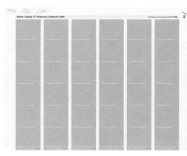

Color Chips

ITT Industries Identity Manual

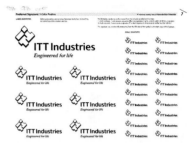

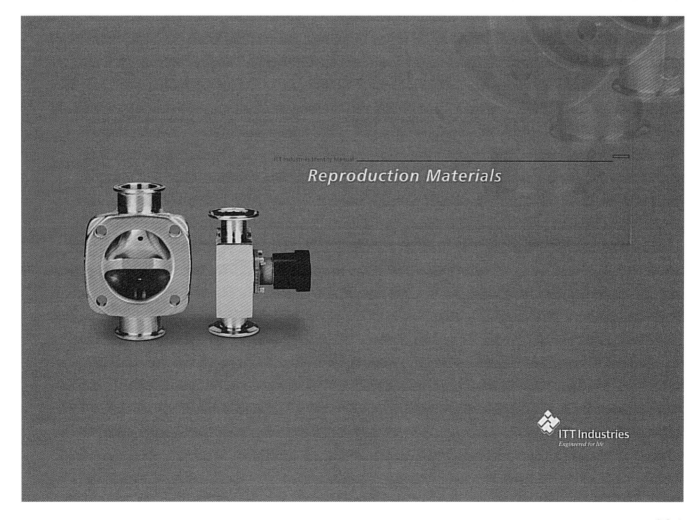

ITT Industries Identity Manual

Reproduction Materials

SIGNAGE/ENVIRONMENTAL GRAPHICS

Client
Legoland
Design Firm
Graphic Solutions
Designers
Frank Mando, Dan Adams, Mike Wosika,
Artemisa Zuazo, John Bushnell, J.D.

Client
Oxmoor Center
Design Firm
TrueNorth
Designers
Ann Swope,
Karen Abney,
Doreen Dehart

Client
SYUFI Enterprises
Design Firm
Graphic Solutions
Designers
Frank Mando, Dan Adams, Artemisa
Zuazo, Mike Wosika, John Bushnell

Client
Commonwealth Convention Center
Design Firm
TrueNorth
Designers
Ann Swope, Karen Abney,
Stephen Brown

Client
  Hunan Garden–Chinese Restaurant

Design Firm
  Bruce Yelaska Design

Designer
  Bruce Yelaska

Client
  Integral Foods

Design Firm
  The DuPuis Group

Designer
  Steven DuPuis

Client
  Woodruff Arts Center

Design Firm
  Lorenc + Yoo Design

Designers
  Jan Lorenc, Chung Youl Yoo, Steve McCall

Client
  Mos Burger

Design Firm
  Design Forum

Designers
  Dave Pinter, Vivienne Padilla, Scott Jeffrey

205

Client
Georgia Center for Children

Design Firm
Lorenc + Yoo Design

Designer
Jan Lorenc

Client
Target Stores

Design Firm
Design Guys

Designers
Lynette Erickson-Sikora, Steven Sikora, Gary Patch

Client
Simon Property Group

Design Firm
Communication Arts, Inc.

Project Manager
Margaret Sewell

Designers
Bryan Gough, Carl Okazaki

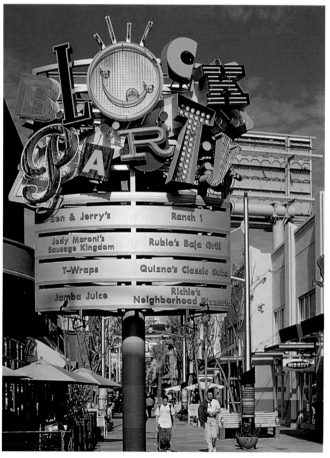

Client
The Mills Corporation

Design Firm
Communication Arts, Inc.

Project Manager
John Ward

Designers
Dave Dute, Jim Redington

Client
  The Mills Corporation

Design Firm
  Kiku Obata and Company

Designers
  Kiku Obata, Kevin Flynn, AIA, Dennis Hyland, AIA, Denise Fuehne,
  Nik Hite, Jennifer Baldwin, John Scheffel, Teresa Norton-Young,
  Kathleen Robert, Carole Jerome, Gen Obata, Jeff Rifkin

Client
  Hines

Design Firm
  Lorenc and Yoo Design

Designers
  Jan Lorenc, Steve McCall

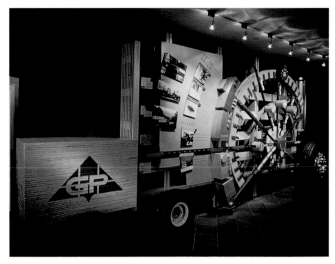

Client
  Georgia-Pacific Corp

Design Firm
  Lorenc and Yoo Design

Designers
  Jan Lorenc, Gary Flesher

Client
  First Union Management

Design Firm
  Lorenc and Yoo Design

Designers
  Jan Lorenc, David Park, Steve McCall

Client
Deutsche Telekom

Design Firm
Interbrand

Designers
Interbrand Design Team

Client
Detroit Opera House

Design Firm
Ford and Earl Associates

Designer
Francheska Guerrero

Client
Methodist Hospital

Design Firm
Corbin Design

Designers
Robert Brengman, Jim Harper

Client
Preit/Journey Communications

Design Firm
Lorenc and Yoo Design

Designers
Jan Lorenc, Chung Youl Yoo, Steve McCall

Client
Laser Pacific Media Corporation

Design Firm
Visual Asylum

Designers
Amy Jo Levine, MaeLin Levine

Client
Southeast Texas Regional Planning Commission

Design Firm
Michael Lee Advertising & Design, Inc.

Designers
Michael Lee, Tanya Lee

Client
Northstar Management Co. LLC

Design Firm
CUBE Advertising and Design

Designers
David Chiow, Matt Marino

Client
Organized Living

Design Firm
EAT Advertising and Design

Creative Director
Patrice Jobe

Art Director and Designer
Peggy Reilly

Photographer
Scott Hepler

Copywriter
Wendy Klein

Client
Michael's Grill Restaurant

Design Firm
EAT Advertising and Design

Creative Director
Patrice Jobe

Art Director and Designer
DeAnne Dodd

Client
Fitz's Bottling Co.

Design Firm
Phoenix Creative, St. Louis

Designer
Deborah Finkelstein

Client
Eden Bioscience

Design Firm
Girvin

Designers
Jeff Haach, Jennifer Bartlett

Client
Mirage Resorts for Bellagio

Design Firm
Girvin

Designer
Stephen Pannone

Client
Urban Retail Properties

Design Firm
RTKL Associates Inc./ID8

Client
Mirage Resorts for Bellagio

Design Firm
Girvin

Designer
Stephen Pannone

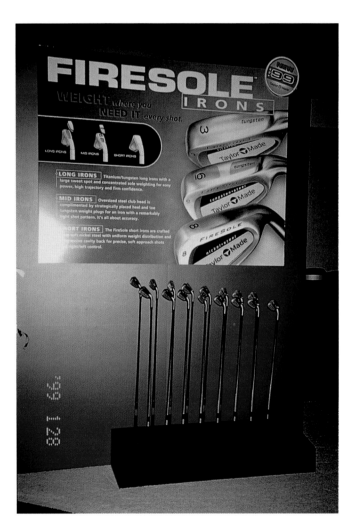

Client
Taylor Made Golf Co.

Design Firm
Laura Coe Design Assoc.

Designers
Denise Heisey, Leanne Leveillee

Client
Novell, Inc.

Design Firm
Hornall Anderson Design Works

Designers
Jack Anderson, Cliff Chung, David Bates, Mike Calkins, Alan Florsheim

Client
Mirage Resorts Inc. for Bellagio

Design Firm
Girvin

Designer
Stephen Pannone

Client
World Wrapps

Design Firm
Girvin

Designers
Jeff Haack, Laurie Vette, Michele Carter

Client
Mirage Resorts for Bellagio

Design Firm
Girvin

Designer
Jeff Haack

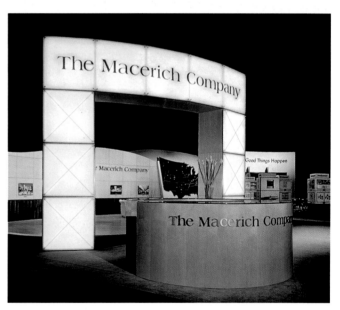

Client
The Macerich Company

Design Firm
TL Horton Design

Designer
Steven Levesque

Client
Georgia State University

Design Firm
Wages Design

Designers
Randy Allison, Joanna Tak

Client
Godiva Chocolatier

Design Firm
Desgrippes Gobé

Design Director
David Ashen

Designer
Leyden Yaeger

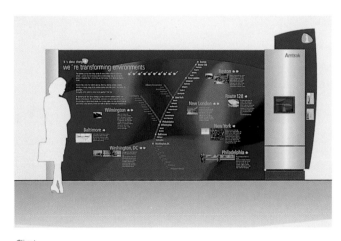

Client
Amtrak

Design Firm
OH&CO in collaboration with IDEO

Creative Director
Brent Oppenheimer

Strategy Director
Robin Haueter

Design Director
Mary Ellen Buttner

Designer
Robert Homack

Copywriter
Ginger Strand

Client
Chelsea Community Hospital

Design Firm
Ford & Earl Associates

Designer
Francheska Guerrero

213

Client
Jones Lang LaSalle
Design Firm
TL Horton Design
Designer
Tony Horton

Client
FANUC Robotics
Design Firm
Ford & Earl Associates
Designers
Joseph Becker, Jerry Kline

Client
Healthline Management
Design Firm
Phoenix Creative, St. Louis
Designer
Steve Wienke
Illustrator
Mary Grandpre

CORPORATE IMAGE BROCHURES

Client
GPCInteractive

Design Firm
Griffith Phillips Creative

Creative Director
Tony Stubbs

Senior Art Director and Designer
Bo McCord

Client
Forrester Research

Design Firm
kor group

Designers
Karen Dendx, Anne Callahan, Jim Gibson

Client
TRW

Design Firm
Gr8

Art Director
Lisa Wurfl-Roeca

Designer
Alain Bolduc

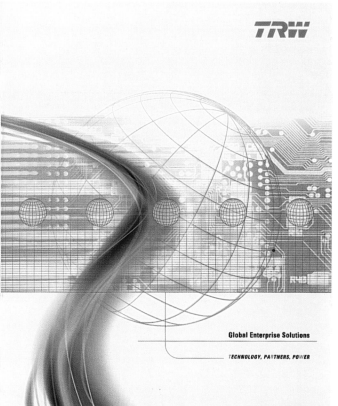

Client
studioluscious

Design Firm
studioluscious

Designers
Susan Hessler, Jennifer Fredritz, Gilberto Albuquerque

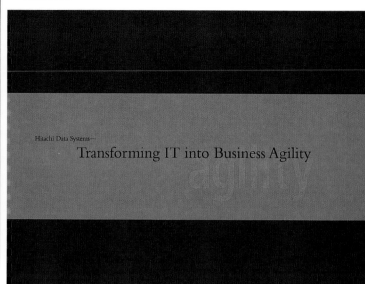

Client
Hitachi Data Systems
Design Firm
Hitachi Data Systems Marketing Communications
Designer
Kim Ocumen

Client
TEK Systems
Art Director
Lisa Wurfl-Roeca

Design Firm
Gr8
Designer
Alain Bolduc

Client
Hawthorne Lane
Design Firm
Hunt Weber Clark Assoc., Inc.
Designers
Jim Decker, Nancy Hunt-Weber

Client
Conrad Properties
Design Firm
Kiku Obata & Company
Designers
Scott Gericke, Jennifer Baldwin, Tom Kowalski

Client
Design Edge

Design Firm
Design Edge

Designer
Jane Brooks

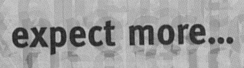

expect more...

Client
Taylor Made Golf Co.

Design Firm
Laura Coe Design Assoc.

Designer
Leanne Leveillee

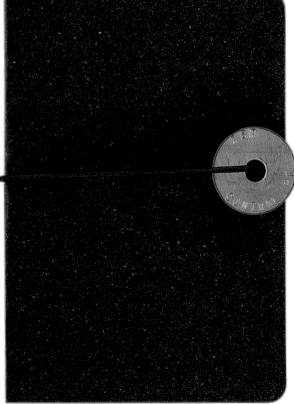

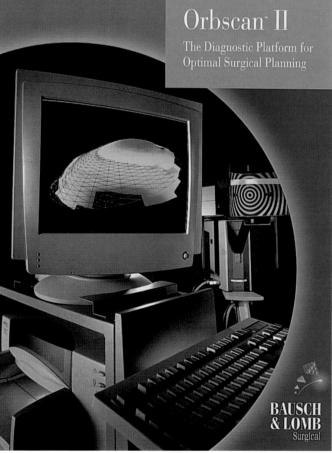

Client
ESM Consulting Engineers

Design Firm
The Traver Company

Designer
Dale Hart

Client
Bausch & Lomb Surgical

Design Firm
The DuPuis Group

Designer
Bill Corridori

Client
Alza Corporation

Design Firm
Casper Design Group

Designer
Christopher Bueler

Client
Toshiba Stroke Research Center

Design Firm
Crowley Webb And Associates

Designers
Mike Lamana, Dion Pender

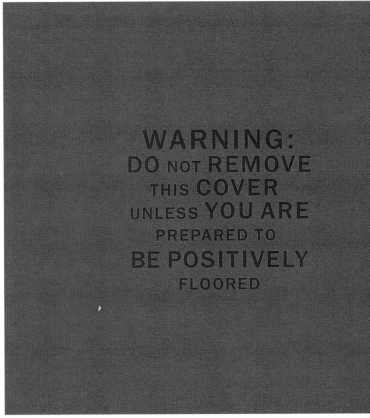

Most people don't know how they're going to die. Donna Wright knew. Her doctor showed her the MRI of her "inoperable" aneurysm. He said it would cause a stroke that would kill her. He called her a "walking time bomb." Donna could have just waited for her life to end. But then she met someone who had a better idea.

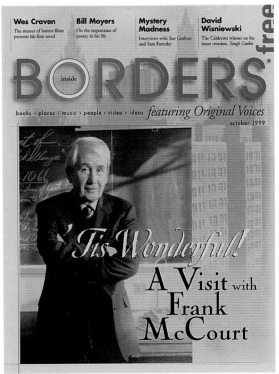

Client
Borders Group, Inc.

Design Firm
Phoenix Creative, St. Louis

Designers
Abigail Twombly, Susan Binns-Roth

WARNING: DO NOT REMOVE THIS COVER UNLESS YOU ARE PREPARED TO BE POSITIVELY FLOORED

Client
Interface Americas

Design Firm
The Valentine Group

Designer
Robert Valentine

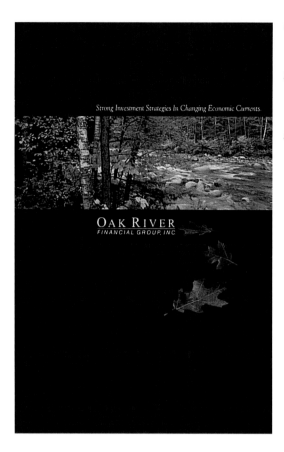

Client
Oak River
Financial
Group, Inc.

Design Firm
**Michael Lee
Advertising
&
Design, Inc.**

Designer
Michael Lee

Landor

Thanksgiving

Branding Program

1999

Client
Landor Associates (Clients)

Design Firm
Landor Associates

Designers
David Weinberger, Wally Krantz

Client
Fusion Specialties

Design Firm
Malowney Associates

Designers
Jennifer Davis, Tracey Ranta, Gene Malowney

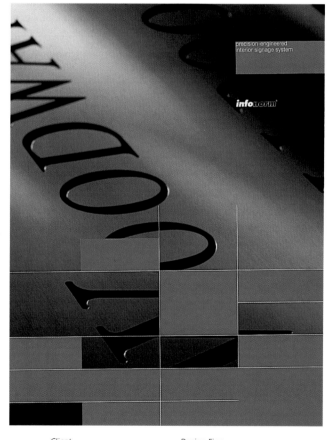

Client
Infonorm Sign Systems

Design Firm
Ford & Earl Associates

Designers
Brian Castle, Bonnie Detloff Zelinski

Client
Matthews Media Group, Inc.

Design Firm
Denver Designs

Designers
Jeffrey L. Dever, Emily Martin Kendall

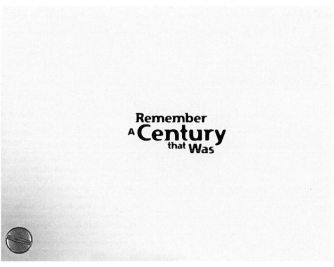

Client
Richard Zeid Design

Design Firm
Richard Zeid Design

Designer
Richard Zeid

Client
Action
Sports
Media

Design Firm
**Jeff Fisher
LogoMotives**

Creative Director
Sara Perrin

Designer
Jeff Fisher

Client
American Express

Design Firm
Cullinane Design

Designer
John Lyness

221

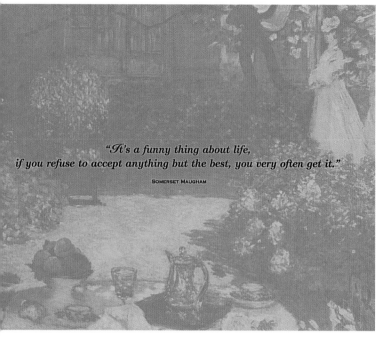

*"It's a funny thing about life,
if you refuse to accept anything but the best, you very often get it."*

SOMERSET MAUGHAM

Client
FCS, Inc.

Design Firm
FCS, Inc.

Designers
Jackie Green, Frank Fisher, Rebecca Shock

Client   Design Firm   Art Director   Designer
ICI Mutual   **Gr8**   Morton Jackson   Rob Rhinehart

Client
Open Systems Advisors

Design Firm
Phillips Design Group

Creative Director
Steve Phillips

Senior Designer
Alison Goudrealt

CROSS ROADS

1001 The Intersection of Business and Technology 00110010101

Un

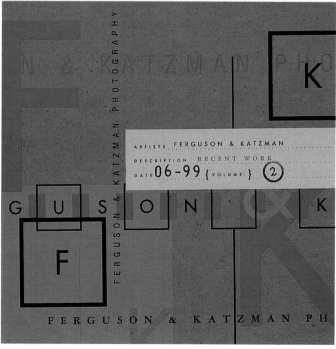

Client   Design Firm
Ferguson & Katzman Photography   **Phoenix Creative, St. Louis**

                                                Designer
                                                Deborah Finkelstein

Client
Keller & Heckman, LLP

Design Firm
Jill Tanenbaum Graphic Design

Designers
Jill Tanenbaum, Leah Germann

Client
Borders, Inc.

Design Firm
Phoenix Creative, St. Louis

Designers
Steve Wienke, Deborah Finkelstein

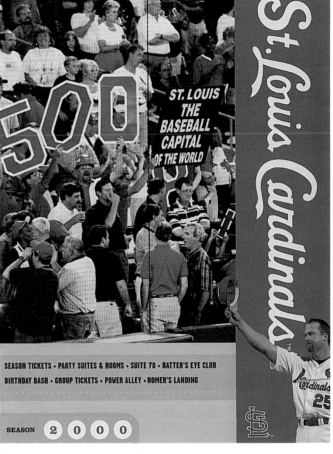

Client
St. Louis Cardinals

Design Firm
Phoenix Creative, St. Louis

Art Director
Paul Jarvis

Designer
Eric Baldwin

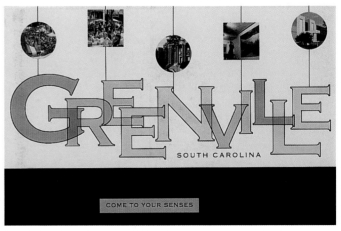

Client
Greenville SC Convention & Visitors Bureau

Design Firm
Sayles Graphic Design

Designer
John Sayles

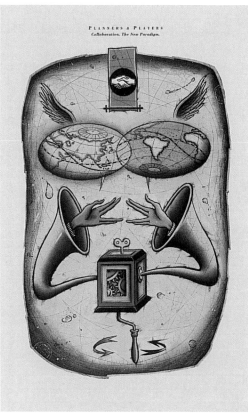

Client
    Paradigm
    Business
    Solutions

Design Firm
    LoBue
    Creative

Designer
    Gary LoBue, Jr.

Client
    Baker Petrolite

Design Firm
    Marion Graphics, L.C.

Designers
    Marion Graphics, L.C.

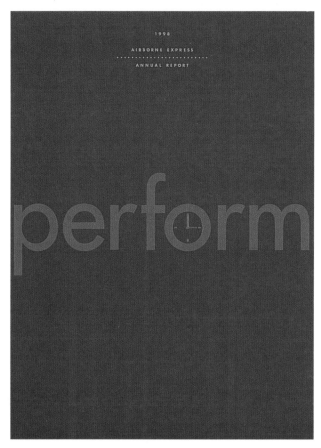

Client
    CNN International

Design Firm
    Ford & Earl Associates

Designer
    Brian Castle

Client
    Airborne Express

Design Firm
    Hornall Anderson Design Works

Designers
    John Hornall, Lisa Cerveny, Bruce Branson-Meyer,
    Jana Nishi, Robb Anderson, Michael Brugman

Client
Allsteel

Design Firm
Michael Orr + Associates, Inc.

Designers
Michael R. Orr,
Thomas Freeland

Client
Unicom

Design Firm
DHI Visual Communication

Designer
Martin Regan

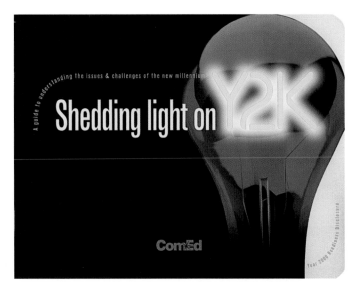

Client
Katten Muchin Zavis

Design Firm
Crosby Associates Inc.

Designers
Bart Crosby, Margorzata Sobus

Client
Astound

Design Firm
Duncan/Channon

Designer
Jacquie Van Keuren

Client
Organizational Dynamics

Design Firm
Stewart Monderer Design, Inc.

Designers
Joseph La Roche, Stewart Monderer

Client
Excelsior-Henderson

Design Firm
Foley Sackett

Designer
Michelle Willinganz

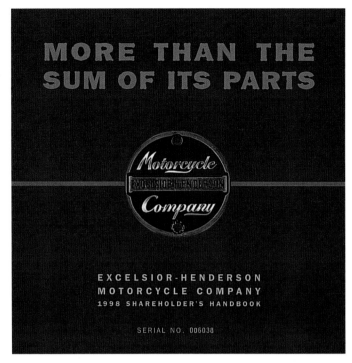

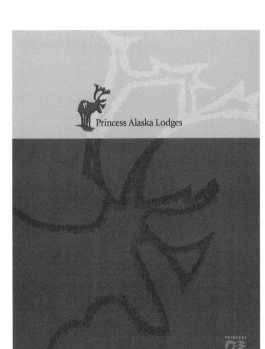

Client
Princess Tours

Design Firm
Belyea

Designers
Patricia Belyea,
Naomi Murphy

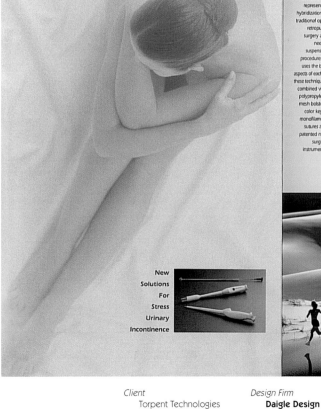

Client
Torpent Technologies

Design Firm
Daigle Design

Designers
Candace Daigle, Jim Ault, Gloria Chen, Paul Dunning

Client
    Primary Color

Design Firm
    FUSE

Designers
    Russell Pierce, Ludovic Bainvel

Client
    Crescent Heights

Design Firm
    Arias Associates

Designers
    Steve Mortensen, Stephanie Yee, Maral Sarkis

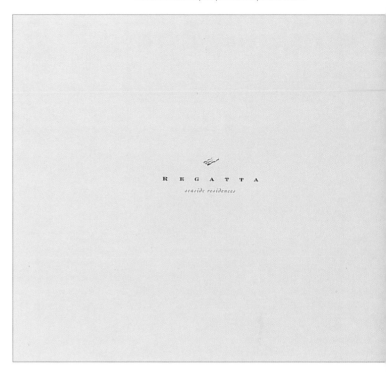

Client
    The Oakland Athletics

Design Firm
    Stratford Design

Designer
    Silvia Stephenson

Photographer
    Michael Zagaris

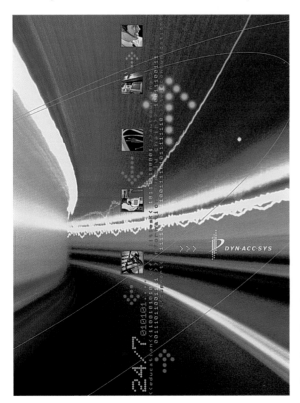

Client
    DynAccSys

Design Firm
    Gr8

Art Director
    Lisa Wurfl-Roeca

Designer
    Alain Bolduc

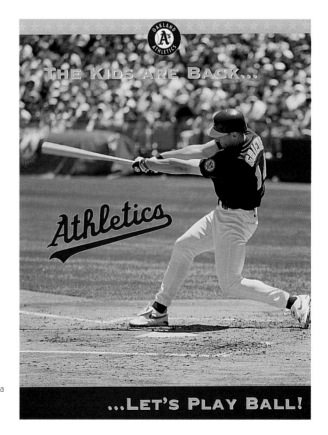

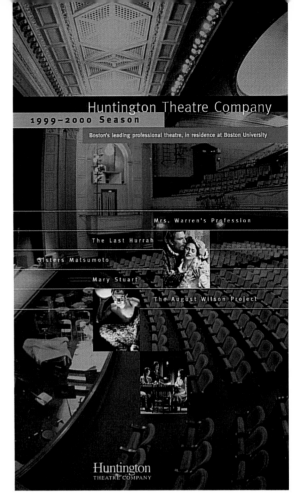

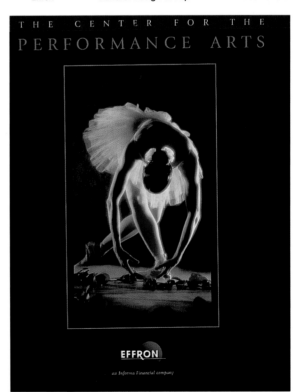

ONE powerful, integrated e-business platform

BRIGHTSTAR

COUNTLESS opportunities for strategic gain

Client
BrightStar

Design Firm
Mortensen Design

Art Director and Designer
Gordon Mortensen

Illustrator
Craig Frazier

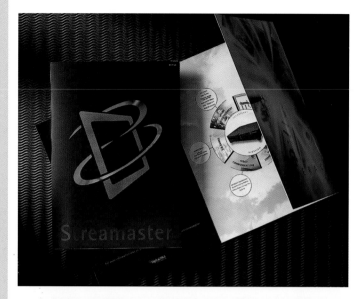

Client
Motorola

Design Firm
McNulty & Co.

Creative Director
Dan McNulty

Designer
Brian Jacobson

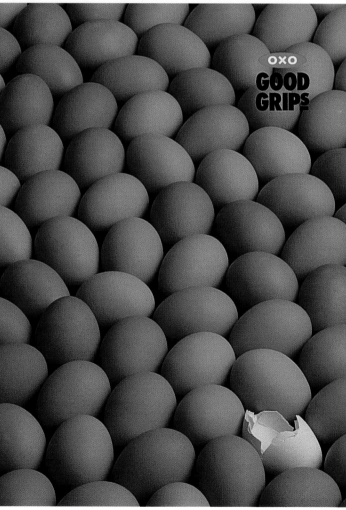

OXO
GOOD GRIPS

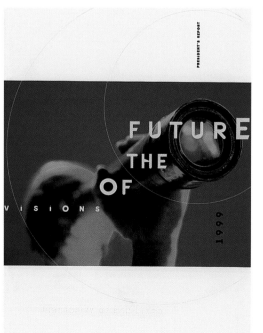

Client
The
University
of
San Diego

Design Firm
**Visual
Asylum**

Designers
MaeLin Levine,
Amy Jo Levine,
Joel Sotelo

Client
OXO International

Design Firm
OXO International's In-House Art Dept.

Art Director and Designer
Jennifer Mariotti Williams

229

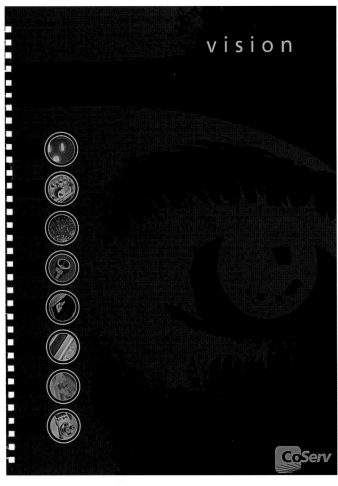

Client
ICI Mutual

Design Firm
Gr8

Art Director
Morton Jackson

Designer
Rob Rhinehart

Client
Dark Horse Productions

Design Firm
Kendall Creative Shop

Designers
Mark K. Platt, Tim Childress

Client
The Creative Center

Design Firm
Dotzler Creative Arts

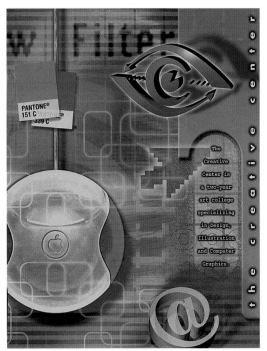

Client
Hitachi
Data
Systems

Design Firm
**Hitachi
Data
Systems
Marketing
Communications**

Designer
Michael McCann

230

Client
The Valentine Group

Design Firm
The Valentine Group

Designer
Robert Valentine

EVERY DAY IS VALENTINE'S DAY

17 VESTRY ST NEW YORK NY 10013   212 925 3103   FAX 212 925 3499

Client
Decrane Aircraft Holdings, Inc.

Design Firm
Willis Advertising

Designer
Ashley Cunningham

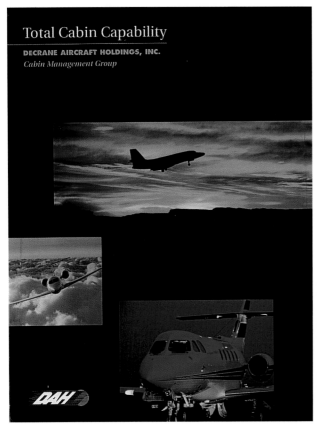

Total Cabin Capability

DECRANE AIRCRAFT HOLDINGS, INC.
Cabin Management Group

Client
Taylor Made Golf Co.

Design Firm
Laura Coe Design Assoc

Designers
Ryoichi Yotsumoto, Leanne Leveillee

Client
Latina Publications

Design Firm
Spring Design Group, Inc.

Designers
Virna Gonzalez
Stuart Lowitt

Client
St. Paul's Episcopal Day School

Design Firm
EAT Advertising and Design

Creative Director
Patrice Jobe

Art Director and Designer
Peggy Reilly

Photographer
Steve Curtis

Client
IBM

Design Firm
Leopard

Designers
Brendan Hemp, Chad Nelson, Andy Rahl

Client
The University of California

Design Firm
Visual Asylum

Designers
Gabriela Ramirez,
Amy Jo Levine, MaeLin Levine

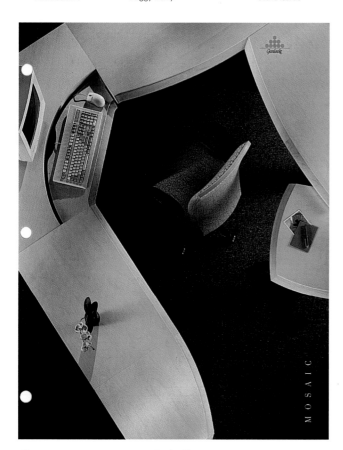

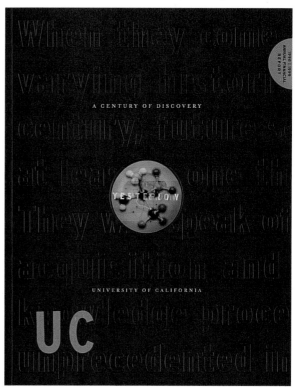

Client
The Gunlocke Company

Design Firm
Michael Orr + Associates, Inc.

Designers
Michael R. Orr, Thomas Freeland

Client
McElveney + Palozzi Design Group, Inc.

Design Firm
McElveney + Palozzi Design Group, Inc.

Designers
Jon Westfall, William McElveney, Steve Palozzi

Client
Fay-Penn Economic Development Council

Design Firm   *Designer*
A to Z communications, inc.   Aimee Lazer

Client
Kansas City Area Development Council

Design Firm
EAT Advertising and Design

Creative Director   *Art Director*
Patrice Jobe   DeAnne Dodd

Designer   *Photographer*
Jeremy Shellhorn   Steve Curtis

Client
DDB
Seattle

Design Firm
**Hornall
Anderson
Design
Works**

Designers
Jack Anderson,
Heidi Favour,
Bruce Branson-Meyer,
Margaret Long

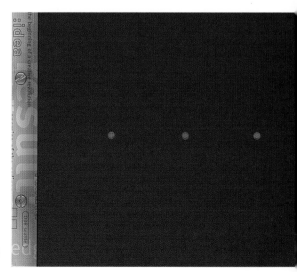

233

Client
Sentient Systems

Design Firm
HC Creative Communications

Designers
Marty Ittner,
Howard Clare

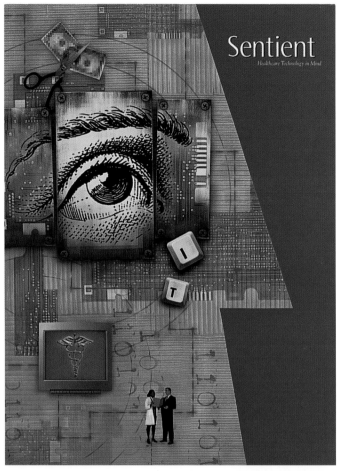

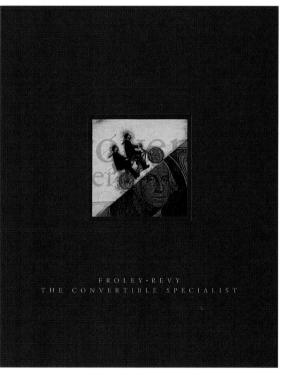

Client
ProBusiness Services

Design Firm
Casper Design Group

Designers
Bill Ribar,
Jessica Lee

Client
Froley-Revy

Design Firm
Baker Designed Communications

Designers
Ron Spohn, Gary Baker

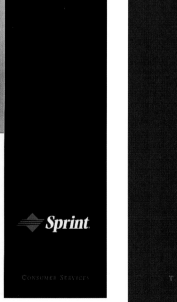

Client
Sprint

Design Firm
EAT Advertising & Design

Creative Director
Patrice Jobe

Art Director
DeAnne Dodd

Designer
Paul Prato

Photographer
Steve Curtis

Client
Massport

Design Firm
kor group

Designers
Anne Callahan, Jim Gibson

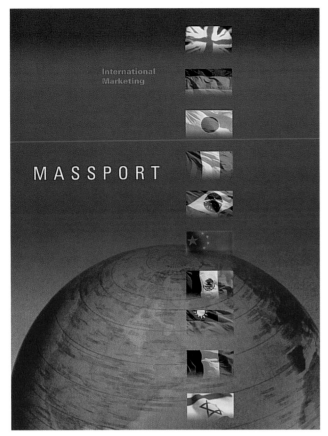

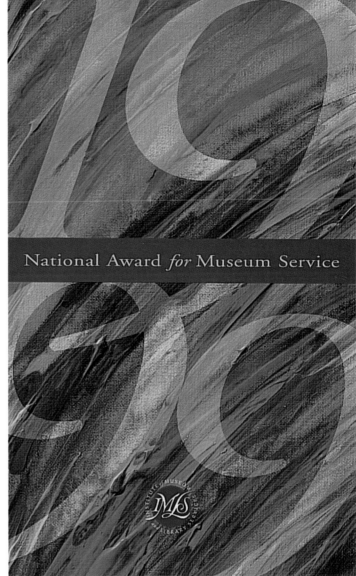

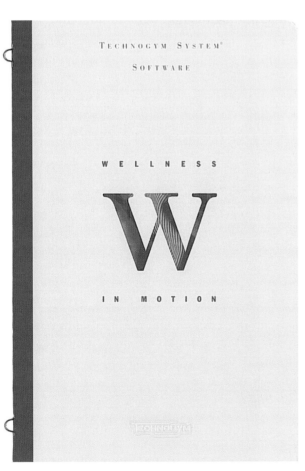

Client
TechnoGym, USA Corp.

Design Firm
Hornall Anderson Design Works

Designers
Jack Anderson, Larry Anderson,
Mary Hermes, Mary Chin Hutchison

Client
Institute of Museum and Library Services

Design Firm
Dever Designs

Designers
Emily Martin Kendall, Christine Draughn

Client
FUSE

Design Firm
FUSE

Designer
Russell Pierce

Client
Hyperion

Design Firm
Landor Associates

Designers
Robert Schroeder,
Robert Matza

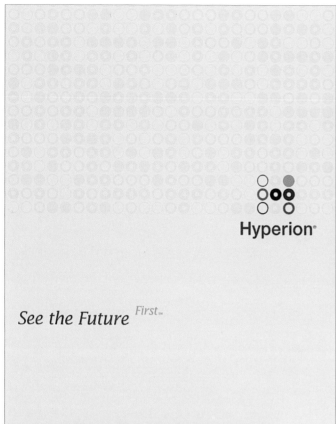

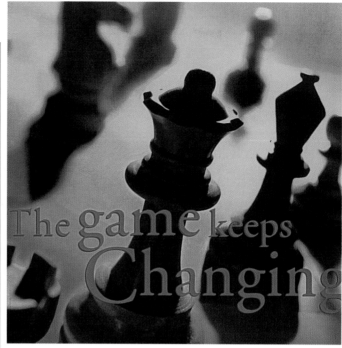

Client
IBAA Community Banking Network

Design Firm
Dever Designs

Designers
Jeffrey L. Dever, Amy White Sucherman

Client
Sunrise
Capital
Partners

Design Firm
**Julia Tam
Design**

Designer
Julia Tam

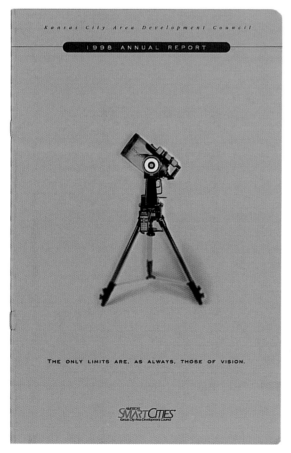

Client
The
Kansas
City
Area
Development
Council

Design Firm
**EAT
Advertising
&
Design**

Creative Director
Patrice Jobe

Art Director
and Designer
DeAnne Dodd

Photographer
Steve Curtis

Photo Manipulation
Paul Prato

Client
    R.C. Hedreen

Design Firm
    The Traver Company

Designer
    Margo Sepanski

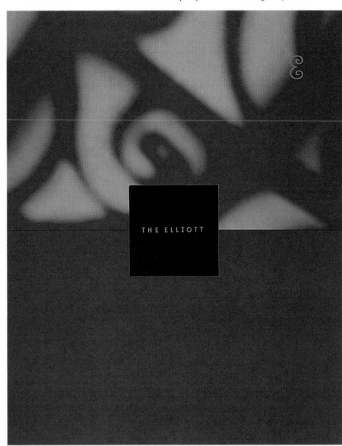

Client
    Institute of Museums and Library Services

Design Firm
    Beth Singer Design

Designers
    Beth Singer, Soung Wiser

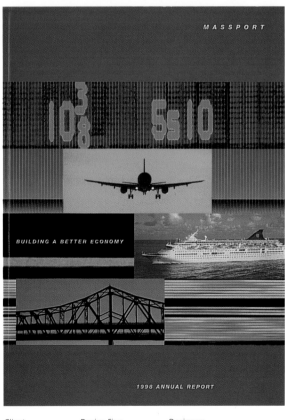

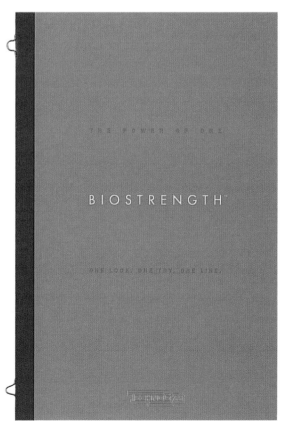

Client
    Massport

Design Firm
    kor group

Designers
    Anne Callahan, Jim Gibson

Client
    TechnoGym,
    USA Corp.

Design Firm
    **Hornall
    Anderson
    Design
    Works**

Designers
    Jack Anderson,
    Larry Anderson,
    Mary Chin Hutchison

WE LIVE HERE.

[4 portraits]

THE CALIFORNIA ENDOWMENT
1998-1999 Annual Report

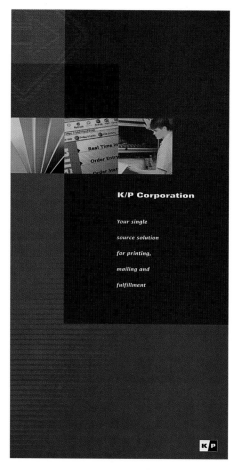

Client
KP Printing

Design Firm
Belyea

Designers
Patricia Belyea,
Ron Lars Hansen

K/P Corporation

*Your single
source solution
for printing,
mailing and
fulfillment*

K|P

Client
The California Endowment

Design Firm
Casper Design Group

Designers
Bill Ribar, Jessica Lee

PEOPLE Soft

Partnership

PeopleSoft
1998 Corporate Report

Client
PeopleSoft

Design Firm
**Casper
Design
Group**

Designer
Christopher Buehler

Client
Leatherman
Tool
Group

Design Firm
**Hornall
Anderson
Design
Works**

Designers
Jack Anderson,
Lisa Cerveny,
David Bates,
Alan Florsheim

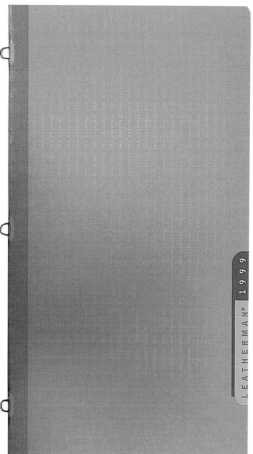

LEATHERMAN 1999

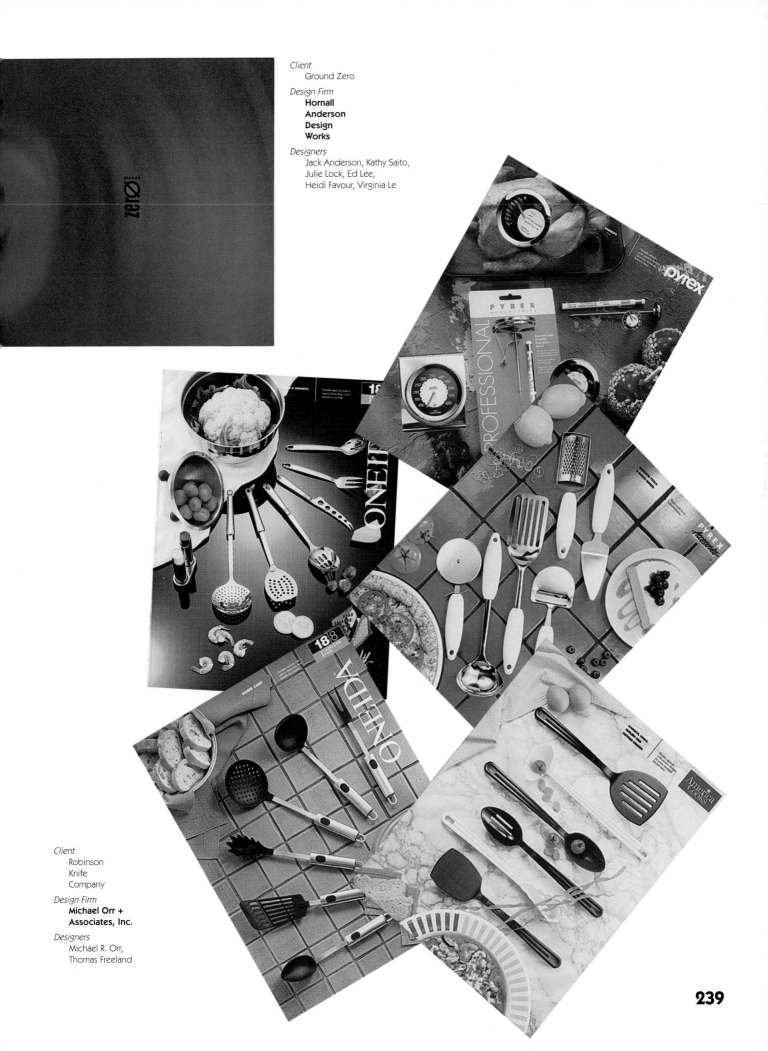

Client
Ground Zero

Design Firm
**Hornall
Anderson
Design
Works**

Designers
Jack Anderson, Kathy Saito,
Julie Lock, Ed Lee,
Heidi Favour, Virginia Le

Client
Robinson
Knife
Company

Design Firm
**Michael Orr +
Associates, Inc.**

Designers
Michael R. Orr,
Thomas Freeland

239

Client
Cracker Barrel

Design Firm
Phoenix Creative, St. Louis

Designer
Caroline Huth

Client
Novell, Inc.

Design Firm
Hornall Anderson Design Works

Designers
Jack Anderson, Larry Anderson, Debra McCloskey,
Jana Wilson Esser, Mary Chin Hutchison, Darlin Gray

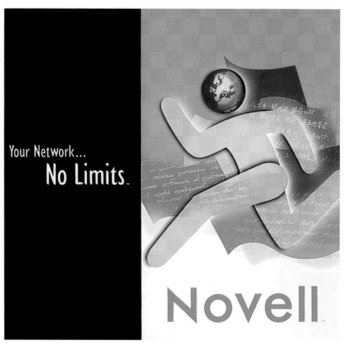

Client
TRW

Art Director
Lisa Wurfl-Roeca

Design Firm
Gr8

Designer
Alain Bolduc

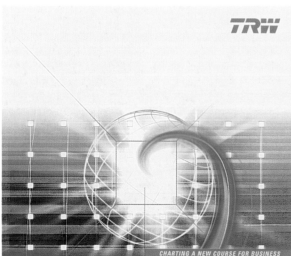
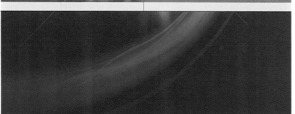

Client
Young & Rubicam

Design Firm
Landor Associates

Designers
Martine Channon, Merel Matzinger

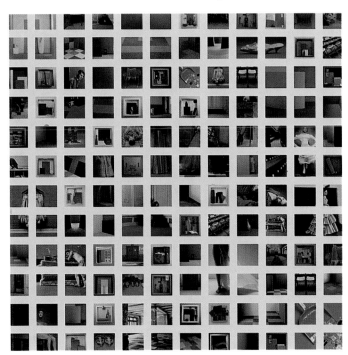

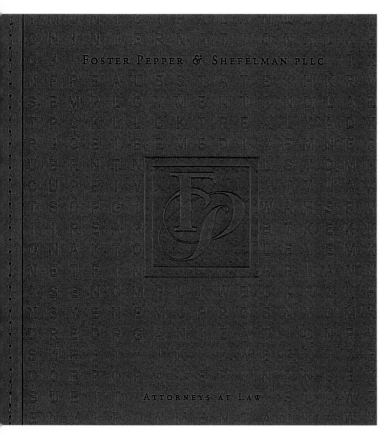

Client
Foster Pepper Shefelman

Design Firm
Hornall Anderson Design Works

Designers
John Hornall, Katha Dalton, Mary Hermes,
Stephanie Lorig, Alan Copeland, Michael Brugman

Client	Design Firm	Designer
CSC	**CSC In-House Design**	Roy Juan

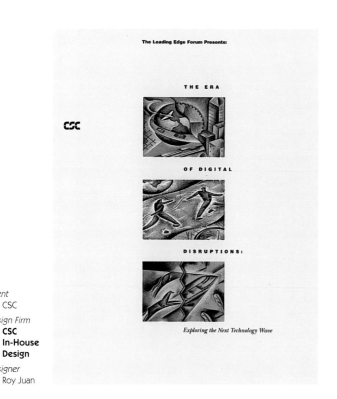

Client
CSC

Design Firm
CSC In-House Design

Designer
Roy Juan

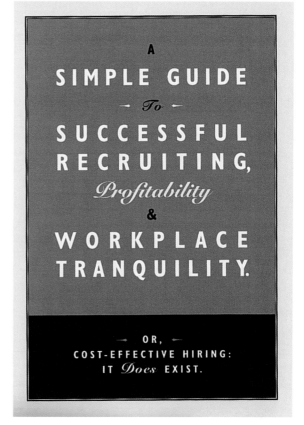

Client	Design Firm	Designer
Search Connection	**Cornerstone**	Jack Hovey

242

TRADEMARK/LOGO DESIGNS

Client
Inktomi

Design Firm
Visigy

Designers
Linda Kelley, Tom Lamar

Client
Mind-Bender.com

Design Firm
Kendall Creative Shop

Designers
Tim Childress, Mark K. Platt

Client
Just Give.org

Design Firm
Diesel Design

Designers
Amy Bainbridge, Luis Dominguez

Client
Staley Builders

Design Firm
Streamline Graphics

Designers
Michael Drane, William Brohard

Client
Accompany

Design Firm
Diesel Design

Designer
Aaron Morton

Client
Visigy

Design Firm
Visigy

Designers
Chris Ardito, Linda Kelley, Chelsea Hernandez

Client
eguana.com

Design Firm
Design Room

Designers
Chad Gordon, Kevin Rathge

THE POWER OF 3

Client
South Trust Bank

Design Firm
DSI/LA

Designers
Scott Hodgin, Benji Fromenthal

Client
Gators' Restaurant

Design Firm
RockMorris Design

Designer
Rock Morris

Client
ViComp Systems, Inc.

Design Firm
Partners & Simons, Inc.

Designer
Lori Saumeri

SouthTrustFunds
It's about trust.^{SM}

Client
South Trust Bank

Design Firm
DSI/LA

Designer
Scott Hodgin

Client
uReach.com

Design Firm
Fuszion Art + Design

Designers
Steve Dreyer, Anthony Fletcher,
Richard Lee Heffner

Client
Codar
Ocean Sensors

Design Firm
Gunion Design

Designer
Jefrey Gunion

Client
Pairgain

Design Firm
Fuse

Designer
Russell Pierce

Client
Dashworks

Design Firm
Streamline Graphics

Designer
Michael Drake

Client
Mediaplex

Design Firm
**Kendall
Creative Shop**

Designer
Mark K. Platt

245

Client
Interactive Learning Group

Design Firm
Hedstrom/Blessing Inc.

Designer
Pamela Goebel

Client
Dental
Concepts

Design Firm
**Handler
Design Group**

Designer
Bruce Handler

Client
Frontier Steel Company

Design Firm
Crowley Webb And Associates

Designer
Dion Pender

Client
i thought

Design Firm
KKD

Designer
Karl Kromer

Client
Potomac
Floor Covering, Inc.

Design Firm
Lomangino Studio Inc.

Designer
Arthur Hsu

Client
McMahon and Cardillo

Design Firm
**Kendra Power Design
& Communication**

Designer
Matthew Wensei

Client
Info Works

Design Firm
**Diesel
Design**

Designer
Aaron Morton

Client
Interactive Learning Group

Design Firm
Hedstrom/Blessing Inc.

Designer
Mike Goebel

246

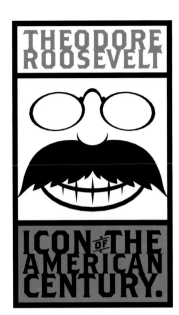

Client
Buffalo and
Erie County
Historical Society

Design Firm
**Crowley Webb
And Associates**

Designers
David Buck,
Sarah Jones,
Rob Wyne

Client
AIGA/Cleveland

Design Firm
Flourish

Designer
Jing Lauengco

Client
Places To Go!

Design Firm
**Phoenix Creative,
St. Louis**

Designer
Ed Mantels-Seeker

Client
Harrison's

Design Firm
Porcelli Design

Designer
Lael Porcelli

Client
Les Piafs

Design Firm
Belyea

Designers
Patricia Belyea, Christian Salas

Client
Ordinary Heroes

Design Firm
**Crowley Webb
And Associates**

Designer
Ann Casady

247

HAUTe DECOR .COM

Client
Haute Decor.com
Design Firm
Tom Fowler, Inc.
Designers
Thomas G. Fowler,
Elizabeth P. Ball

@cafe.com

Client
Novell, Inc.
Design Firm
**Hornall Anderson
Design Works**
Designers
Jack Anderson, Cliff Chung,
David Bates, Larry Anderson,
Sonja Max, Mike Calkins

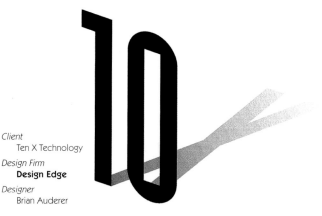

Client
Ten X Technology
Design Firm
Design Edge
Designer
Brian Auderer

eventra

Client
Eventra
Design Firm
Tom Fowler, Inc.
Designer
Karl S. Maruyama

workengine™

Client
Gettuit.com
Design Firm
**Hornall Anderson
Design Works**
Designers
Jack Anderson, Gretchen Cook, James Tee, Julie Lock, Henry Yiu

iNEIGHBORS.COM

Client
Reynolds and Rose
Design Firm
Tom Fowler, Inc.
Designers
Karl S. Maruyama

Tenet Educational Network

Client
Tenet Healthcare
Design Firm
Baker Designed Communications
Designers
Brian Keenan, Gary Baker

ibc

Interactive Brand Center

Client
IBC
Design Firm
Tom Fowler, Inc.
Designer
Elizabeth P. Ball

Client
Ecast
Design Firm
Tsuchiya Sloneker Communications
Creative Director
Julie Tsuchiya
Designer
Amy Harding

Client
McCaw
Design Firm
**Hornall Anderson
Design Works**
Designers
Jack Anderson,
Margaret Long

Client
Tenet Healthcare
Design Firm
Baker Designed Communications
Designer
Gary Baker

Katten | Muchin | Zavis

K | M | Z

Client
Katten Muchin Zavis
Design Firm
Crosby Associates Inc.
Designer
Bart Crosby

Client
Wells Fargo
Design Firm
Hornall Anderson Design Works
Designers
Jack Anderson, Kathy Saito, Alan Copeland

Client
Hanley-Wood, Inc.
Design Firm
**William J. Kircher
& Associates, Inc.**
Designer
Bruce E. Morgan

**HAMPTON
FINANCIAL
PARTNERS**

Client
Hampton Financial Partners
Design Firm
Triad, Inc.
Designer
Michael Dambrowski

Client
Powerware Solutions
Design Firm
Stratford Design
Designer
Tim Gerould

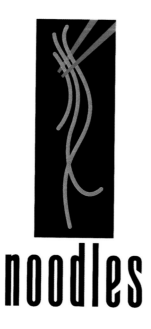

Design Firm
Girvin

Creative Director
John Shadler

Art Director
Stephen Pannone

Designer
Erich Schreck

Client
The Double Eagle

Design Firm
Weller Institute

Designer
Don Weller

Client
Kimpton Hotel
& Restaurant Group

Design Firm
**Hunt Weber Clark
Assoc., Inc.**

Designers
Jim Deeken,
Nancy Hunt-Weber

Client
Moonlight Mushrooms

Design Firm
A to Z Communications, inc.

Client
Zoë Restaurant

Design Firm
John Kneapler Design

Designers
John Kneapler, Matt Waldman

Client
Whale's Tale

Design Firm
Malowany Associates

Designer
Gene Malowany

Client
Mirage Resorts for Bellagio

Design Firm
Girvin

Designer
Stephen Pannone

Client
Pierce
Chemical Company

Design Firm
Reed Sendecke, Inc.

Designer
Design Staff of
Reed Sendecke, Inc.

Design Firm
Sign Here, Inc.

Designer
Lori Reynolds

Client
Doubletree Hotel Dayton Downtown

Design Firm
Five Visual Communication & Design

Designers
Denny Fagan, Rondi Tschopp

Client
Hanes

Design Firm
Interbrand Gerstman & Meyers

Designers
Mitch Gottlieb, Annie Baker, Jillian Mazzacano

Client
China World
Hotel Beijing

Design Firm
Arias Associates

Designers
Mauricio Arias,
Stephanie Yee

Verandah Cafe

Client
Doubletree Hotel Dayton Downtown

Design Firm
Five Visual Communication & Design

Designers
Denny Fagan, Rondi Tschopp

Client
Boostworks

Design Firm
Duncan/Channon

Designer
Jacquie VanKeuren

251

Client
Bank of Petaluma

Design Firm
Mortensen Design

Art Director
Gordon Mortensen

Designers
Gordon Mortensen,
Wendy Chon

BANK OF PETALUMA

NANCY**LOPEZ**GOLF™

Client
Nancy Lopez Golf

Design Firm
Miriello Grafico, Inc.

Designer
Courtney Mayer

Client
Eazel

Design Firm
Mortensen Design

Art Director
Gordon Mortensen

Designer
PJ Nidecker

DUNGENESS RIVER CENTER
at Railroad Bridge Park

Client
Rainshadow
Natural Science
Foundation

Design Firm
**Laurel Black
Design**

Designer
Laurel Black

Client
Knowledge Garage

Design Firm
Boelts Bros. Assoc.

Designers
E. Boelts, E. Taylor,
J. Boelts, K. Stratford

Client
MyPlay, Inc.

Design Firm
**Mortensen
Design**

Art Director
Gordon Mortensen

Designer
PJ Nidecker

Client
Quisic.com

Design Firm
Jensen Design Associates

Designer
David Jensen

springboard

Client
Handspring, Inc.

Design Firm
Mortensen Design

Art Director
Gordon Mortensen

Designer
PJ Nidecker

252

Client
Malt Whiskey.com

Design Firm
Shields Design

Designer
Charles Shields

Client
New Hope Church

Design Firm
Wages Design

Designer
Joanna Tak

HEBERGER
&COMPANY
Certified Public Accountants

Client
Heberger & Company, Inc.

Design Firm
Shields Design

Designer
Charles Shields

Client
Big Score

Design Firm
Duncan/Channon

Designer
Jacquie VanKeuren

Streamaster

microlink

Client
Motorola

Design Firm
McNulty & Co.

Creative Director
Dan McNulty

Designer
Brian Jacobson

Client
Microlink

Design Firm
Miriello Grafico, Inc.

Designer
Chris Keeney

Client
Lumen

Design Firm
Stratford Design

Designer
Tim Gerould

Client
Mercer

Design Firm
Stratford Design

Designer
Tim Gerould

Client
Beals Martin

Design Firm
Stratford Design

Designers
G.W. Stratford, Tim Gerould

Slinging Star

Client
Slinging Star Productions

Design Firm
Stratford Design

Designer
Tim Gerould

Client
icf

Design Firm
Stratford Design

Designer
Silvia Stephenson

Client
Design Online

Design Firm
David Lemley Design

Designers
David Lemley, Emma Wilson

Client
Kindercotton

Design Firm
Stratford Design

Designer
Silvia Stephenson

Client
Cromatica
Laser Applications

Design Firm
Pandora

Designer
Silvia Grossmann

Client
Glenborough

Design Firm
Stratford Design

Designers
G.W. Stratford, Sr.,
Silvia Stephenson,
Tim Gerould

The Computer Skills Network

Client
Warner Lambert

Design Firm
Taylor Design

Designer
Ann Obringer

254

Client
Stone Ridge
Shopping Center

Design Firm
Rubber Design

Designer
Jacquie VanKeuren

Client
Pony Xpresso

Design Firm
Design Edge

Designer
Jane Brooks

gettuit.com™

Client
Gettuit.com

Design Firm
**Hornall Anderson
Design Works**

Designers
Jack Anderson,
Kathy Saito,
Gretchen Cook,
James Tee,
Julie Lock,
Henry Yiu

The Remote Access Software Solution!

Client
Cisco Systems

Design Firm
Stratford Design

Designers
G.W. Stratford, Sr., Tim Gerould, Rebecca Lambing

Client
Good Morning
Investments

Design Firm
**Crosby
Associates Inc.**

Designer
Bart Crosby

Client
Rittenhouse Optical

Design Firm
**Zeewy Design
[and] Marketing Communications**

Designers
Lia Cautoun, Orly Zeewy

255

advertising.com

Client
Advertising.com

Design Firm
Taylor Design

Designer
Daniel Taylor

UNITED WAY®
OF THE BAY AREA

Client
The United Way
of the Bay Area

Design Firm
SBG Enterprises

Designers
Mark Bergman,
Richard Patterson

ANGELES VENTURES

Client
Angeles Ventures

Design Firm
Art Director (Doug Boyd)

Art Director
Doug Boyd

handspring

Client
Handspring, Inc.

Design Firm
Mortensen Design

Art Director
Gordon Mortensen

Designer
PJ Nidecker

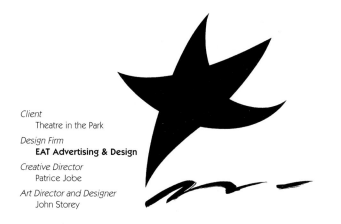

Client
Theatre in the Park

Design Firm
EAT Advertising & Design

Creative Director
Patrice Jobe

Art Director and Designer
John Storey

LARCHMONT HEIGHTS
HERITAGE ASSOCIATION

Client
Larchmont
Heights
Heritage
Association

Design Firm
**Haines Wilkerson
Design,
Los Angeles**

Designers
Haines Wilkerson,
Amy Sun

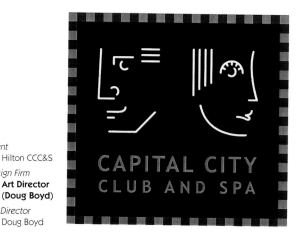

CAPITAL CITY
CLUB AND SPA

Client
Hilton CCC&S

Design Firm
**Art Director
(Doug Boyd)**

Art Director
Doug Boyd

DiPrima
Insurance Specialists

Client
Di Prima Insurance

Design Firm
McNulty & Co.

Designers
Dan McNulty, Eugene Bustillos

Client
Trinity
Building Maintenance

Design Firm
Stratford Design

Designer
John F. Morgan

"Make a Difference"

Client
Fiber Force, Inc.

Design Firm
Sanft Design Inc.

Designer
Alfred C. Sanft

Client
Brown
Shoe
Company

Design Firm
Kiku Obata
& Company

Designers
Scott Gericke,
Amy Knopf,
Joe Floresca,
Jennifer Baldwin

BROWN SHOE

THE VERANDA
COLLECTION

Client
The
Veranda
Collection

Design Firm
Schwener
Design Group

Designer
Diane Schwener

CONCORD℠
MILLS

Client
The Mills Corporation

Design Firm
Kiku Obata & Company

Designer
Kathleen Robert

ART SPACE

Client
The Kansas City Art Institute

Design Firm
EAT Advertising & Design

Art Director and Designer
DeAnne Dodd

METROMEDIA
FIBER NETWORK

Client
Metromedia Fiber Network

Design Firm
Guest Informant Custom Publishing

Creative Director
Haines Wilkerson

Designer
Benjamin Nicolas

rightstart.com

Client
The Right Start

Design Firm
**Art Director
(Doug Boyd)**

Art Director
Doug Boyd

Client
Eastman Kodak Company

Design Firm
Forward

Designers
Jim Forward, Dulce Stofer

ATLANTIS

Client
Atlantis

Design Firm
Pandora

Client
Food Marketing Institute

Design Firm
William J. Kircher & Associates, Inc.

Designer
Bruce E. Morgan

O P T

I C A L

R E F L E

C T I O N S

Client
Optical
Reflections

Design Firm
**Peter Taflan
Marketing
Communications**

Art Director
Janssen Strother

Client
ILP

Design Firm
Boelts Bros. Assoc.

Designers
E. Boelts,
J. Boelts,
K. Stratford,
A. Arriatta

Client
Bagel Bakers

Design Firm
**Nick Kaars
& Associates Inc.**

Designers
Nick Kaars,
Oliver Kinney

Client
WNIN

Design Firm
Fire House, Inc.

Designer
Bob Young

Client
Creative Club of Atlanta

Design Firm
Wages Design

Designer
Bob Wages

Client
Visual Asylum

Design Firm
Visual Asylum

Designers
Joel Sotelo, Lizette Picasso, Amy Jo Levine, MaeLin Levine

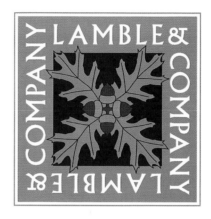

Client
Lamble & Company

Design Firm
Fire House, Inc.

Designer
Bob Young

Client
Telestar Interactive Corporation

Design Firm
Visual Marketing Associates, Inc.

Designer
Tom Davie

Client
Voice Web Corporation

Design Firm
Forward

Designers
Forward

Client
Science
Museum
of Minnesota

Design Firm
Little & Company

Design Director
Michael Lizama

Designers
Michael Lizama, Viet Do

Client
Ridge Creek Ranch

Design Firm
Trudy Cole-Zielanski Design

Designer
Trudy Cole-Zielanski

PAZZALUNA
URBAN TRATTORIA & BAR

Client
Morrisey Hospitality

Design Firm
Little & Company

Design Director
Jim Jackson

Designers
Viet Do, Michael Lizama

Client
A Cut Above Castro

Design Firm
Duncan/Channon

Designer
Jacquie VanKeuren

net radio.com

Client
Netradio.com

Design Firm
Little & Company

Designer Director
Stefan Hartung

Designers
Scott Sorenson, Stefan Hartung

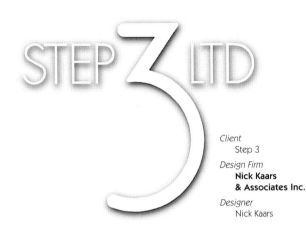

STEP 3 LTD

Client
Step 3

Design Firm
**Nick Kaars
& Associates Inc.**

Designer
Nick Kaars

AGA
American Gas Association

Client
American Gas Association

Design Firm
Dever Designs

Designer
Jeffrey L. Dever

TRATTORIA DEL
Lupo
WOLFGANG PUCK

Client
Wolfgang Puck

Design Firm
**Full Steam
Marketing
& Design**

Designer
Darryl Zimmerman

Client
William J. Kircher & Associates, Inc.

Design Firm
William J. Kircher & Associates, Inc.

Designer
Bruce E. Morgan

CULINARY INSTITUTE OF THE PACIFIC
The University of Hawai'i

Client
University of Hawaii

Design Firm
Eric Woo Design Inc.

Designer
Eric Woo

THE ENCHANTED COTTAGE

Client
The Enchanted Cottage

Design Firm
Guarino Graphics & Design Studio

Designer
Jan Guarino

Client
Hollywood•com/Laurie Silvers

Design Firm
B.D. Fox & Friends Inc. Advertising

Designers
Mary Trainor, Garrett Burke, John Soltis

Client
eMeter

Design Firm
Insight Design Communications

Designers
Sherrie Holdeman, Tracy Holdeman

EAC

EDUCATION & ASSISTANCE CORP

Client
Education
& Assistance Corp.

Design Firm
**Guarino
Graphics & Design
Studio**

Designer
Jan Guarino

Client
gardenandholiday.com

Design Firm
**Insight
Design
Communications**

Designers
Sherrie Holdeman,
Tracy Holdeman

Caredata.com

Client
Caredata

Design Firm
Addison Whitney

Designer
Lori Earnhardt

Client
Comet
Management
Services, Inc.

Design Firm
**Herip
Associates**

Designers
Walter Herip,
Rick Holb,
John Menter

 **SpectrAlliance**

Client
SpectrAlliance, Inc.

Design Firm
CUBE Advertising & Design

Designers
David Chiow, Kevin Hough

Visionael

Client
Visionael Corporation

Design Firm
Halleck

Designer
Wayne Wright

Vast
SOLUTIONS™

Client
Vast
Solutions

Design Firm
**Addison
Whitney**

Designer
Logan Watts

educosm

Client
educosm

Design Firm
Addison Whitney

Designer
Logan Watts

Performix™

Client
Plasti Dip International

Design Firm
Addison Whitney

Designer
Logan Watts

SECOH
SUPPORTING EXCEPTIONAL CITIZENS OF HAWAII

Client
SECOH

Design Firm
Eric Woo Design Inc.

Designer
Eric Woo

Think Outside™

Client
Think Outside

Design Firm
Mires Design

Art Director
John Ball

Designer
Miguel Perez

Client
Value Lite
Engineered Products

Design Firm
Minx Design

Designer
Cecilia M. Sveda

The University's Campaign for Hawai'i

Building Rainbow Bridges

Client
University of Hawaii
Foundation

Design Firm
Eric Woo Design Inc.

Designer
Eric Woo

Client
Intel

Design Firm
Sapient

Designer
Karin Bryant

Client
Jim Barber Studio

Design Firm
Stephen Loges Graphic Design

Designer
Stephen Loges

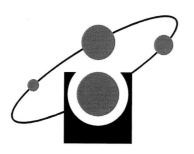

Client
Incube8.com

Design Firm
Gr8

Art Director
Lisa Wurfl-Roeca

Designer
Alain Bolduc

Client
Spring Street

Design Firm
Sapient

Designer
Henrik Olsen

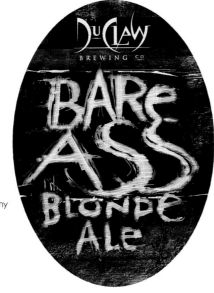

Client
DuClaw Brewing Company

Design Firm
Gr8

Art Director
Lisa Wurfl-Roeca

Designer
Alain Bolduc

Client
Embrace

Design Firm
Gr8

Art Director
Lisa Wurfl-Roeca

Designer
Alain Bolduc

Client
GuesTech, LLC

Design Firm
Gr8

Art Director
Lisa Wurfl-Roeca

Designer
Margaret Pharr

C L E A R *I N S I G H T*
Extraordinary Communication Enablers

Client
Clear Insight

Design Firm
Clear Insight

Designer
Julie Eubanks

Client
DuClaw Brewing Company

Design Firm
Gr8

Art Director
Lisa Wurfl-Roeca

Designer
Alain Bolduc

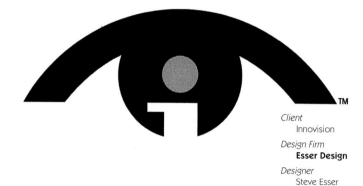

Client
Innovision

Design Firm
Esser Design

Designer
Steve Esser

Client
The Looking Glass Company

Design Firm
Arias Associates

Designers
Mauricio Arias, Stephanie Yee, Marites Algones

Client
Darwin Health

Design Firm
NewIDEAS, Inc.

Designer
Patty O. Seger

Client
Edmunds.com

Design Firm
Gregory Thomas Asso.

Designers
Gregory Thomas, Sabrina L'i

Client
Saint Louis Zoo

Design Firm
CUBE
Advertising & Design

Designers
David Chiow,
Matt Marino

264

Client
Cyber Art

Design Firm
Gill Fishman Associates

Creative Director
Gill Fishman

Designer and Illustrator
Alicia Ozyjowski

Client
Logal.net

Design Firm
Gill Fishman Associates

Creative Director
Gill Fishman

Designer
Alicia Ozyjowski

Illustrator
Michael Persons

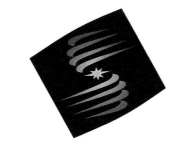

Client
Swift Touch Corp.

Design Firm
Gill Fishman Associates

Creative Director
Gill Fishman

Designer and Illustrator
Alicia Ozyjowski

Client
Telcordia Technologies

Design Firm
Lister Butler Consulting

Senior Designer
William Davis

Client
Saint Louis Zoo

Design Firm
CUBE Advertising & Design

Designers
David Chiow, Kevin Hough

Client
Hawaii Forest Industry Assoc.

Design Firm
Eric Woo Design Inc.

Designer
Eric Woo

Client
Southern Maid Entertainment— Chris Zarpas

Design Firm
B.D. Fox & Friends, Inc., Advertising

Designer
Chris Bartolini

Client
DuClaw Brewing Company

Design Firm
Gr8

Art Director
Lisa-Wurfl-Roeca

Designer
Alain Bolduc

Surebridge

Client
Surebridge Inc.

Design Firm
Gill Fishman Associates

Creative Director
Gill Fishman

Designer and Illustrator
Michael Persons

COLOSSEVM

SINCE 80 A.D.

Design Firm
**Rassman
Design**

Designers
John Rassman,
Amy Rassman,
Lynn D'amato,
Vicki Freeman,
Gwyn Browning

Nexium®
esomeprazole

Client
Astra Zeneca

Design Firm
Interbrand

Designers
Interbrand Design Team

Design Firm
Rassman Design

Designers
John Rassman, Lynn D'amato,
Amy Rassman, Vicki Freeman, Gwyn Browning

Client
Flat 9 Jazz/Funk Trio

Design Firm
Flat 9

Designer
Johnny Gallardo

FIDEL BISTRO

Client
Fidel Bistro

Design Firm
Gardner Design

Designer
Travis Brown

Client
Artifex

Design Firm
Esser Design

Designers
Steve Esser, Don Newland

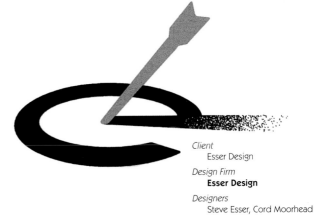

Client
Esser Design

Design Firm
Esser Design

Designers
Steve Esser, Cord Moorhead

Client
Haydon Building Corp.

Design Firm
Esser Design

Designer
Steve Esser

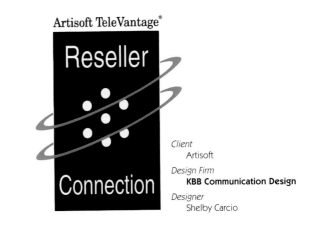

Client
Artisoft

Design Firm
KBB Communication Design

Designer
Shelby Carcio

Client
Pinnacle Health of Massachusetts

Design Firm
KBB Communications Design

Designer
Sue Gordon

Client
fatbrain.com

Design Firm
Interbrand

Designers
Interbrand
Design Team

Client
Quincy Community Action Programs, Inc.

Design Firm
KBB Communications Design

Designer
Anna Bemis

Client
Soma
Foundation

Design Firm
**Artemis
Creative, Inc.**

Designers
Wes Aoki,
Gary Nusinow

267

Client
Soundtec

Design Firm
Walsh Associates

Designer
Kerry Walsh

Client
Internet
Medium Discovery
Group, LLC

Design Firm
Greene
Communications
Design

Designers
Peter Greene,
Hester Greene

Client
NannyBank.com

Design Firm
L. Creighton Dinsmore Design

Designer
L. Creighton Dinsmore

Client
Ansible Software

Design Firm
Greene
Communications Design

Designers
Hester Greene,
Naomi Yamomoto

Client
IPN, Inc.

Design Firm
X Design Company

Designer
Alex Valderrama

Client
Open Art Show

Design Firm
X Design Company

Designers
Alex Valderrama, Amy Adams

Client
American Association
of Engineering Societies

Design Firm
MacVicar
Design
+ Communications

Designer
William A. Gordon

Client
Montauk
Energy Capital

Design Firm
Elias/Savion
Advertising

Designer
Ronnie Savion

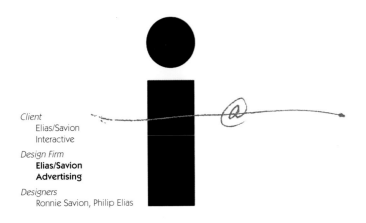

Client
Elias/Savion
Interactive

Design Firm
**Elias/Savion
Advertising**

Designers
Ronnie Savion, Philip Elias

Client
Club Com

Design Firm
Elias/Savion Advertising

Designer
Mimi Rich

Client
Buzzcuts Maximum Lawn Care

Design Firm
Gardner Design

Designer
Bill Gardner

inter SURVEY

Client
interSURVEY

Design Firm
**Partners
& Simons**

Designer
Karen Papplardo

Amtrak·

Client
Amtrak

Design Firm
**OH&CO
in collaboration
with IDEO**

Creative Director
Brent Oppenheimer

Design Director
Mary Ellen Buttner

Client
Powertrax

Design Firm
Mires Design

Art Director
Jose Serrano

Designers
Miguel Perez,
Lucas Salvatierra

Illustrator
Miguel Perez

BOTANICUS

Client
Botanicus

Design Firm
Gibson Creative

Designer
Juliette Brown

Client
Badlanders

Design Firm
Girvin

Designers
Kevin Henderson, Chie Masuyama, Tim Girvin, Sam Knight

Client
iclips.com

Design Firm
Diamant Design

Client
Eden Bioscience

Design Firm
Girvin

Designers
Jeff Haack, Jennifer Bartlett

Client
Pasta Basket Gourmet Gift Baskets

Design Firm
Five Visual Communication & Design

Designer
Rondi Tschopp

Client
The Yellow Pages

Design Firm
Mires Design

Art Directors
Jose Serrano,
Brian Fandetti

Designer and Illustrator
Miguel Perez

HARLEYELLIS

Client
HarleyEllis

Design Firm
Ford & Earl Associates

Designer
Brian Castle

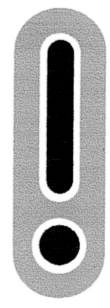

Client
The Marketing Store

Design Firm
The Marketing Store

Designer
Susan Leeson

Cultivations™

Home · Garden · Life

Client
Cultivations

Design Firm
Bailey Design Group, Inc.

Designer
David Fiedler

PASSAGES™

Embracing Change

Client
Passages International

Design Firm
studioluscious

Designer
Jennifer Fredritz

Client
Golf Digest Magazine

Design Firm
McMillian Design

Designer
William McMillian

LINKS FOR LIFE

Client
Dr. Richard Belli, Podiatrist

Design Firm
McMillian Design

Designer
William McMillian

RIVERS OF STEEL

HERITAGE AREA

Client
Rivers of Steel Heritage Area

Design Firm
Adam, Filippo & Associates

Designers
David Zimmerly, Robert Adam

CARABELLA

Client
Carabella

Design Firm
Adam, Filippo & Associates

Designer
David Zimmerly

Coordinated
Care
Network

Client
Coordinated Care Network

Design Firm
Adam, Filippo & Associates

Designer
Robert Adam

ALLEGHENY COUNTY

CHAMBER FEDERATION

Client
Allegheny County Chamber Federation

Design Firm
Adam, Filippo & Associates

Designers
David Zimmerly, Robert Adam

271

distilled images
a picture's worth

SPIRIT FILLED DOGS™

Client
Distilled Images

Design Firm
AERIAL

Designers
Misty Bralver, Tracy Moon

Client
Spirit Filled Dogs

Design Firm
Genghis Design

Designer
Dale Monahan

ENA

Client
Cena Restaurant

Design Firm
John Kneapler Design

Designers
John Kneapler, Chris Dietrich

NUBAR inc.

Client
Nubar, Inc.

Design Firm
Striegal & Associates

Designers
Peggy Striegel, Dustin Staiger

Client
Alamo
Family Foot Care, P.A.

Design Firm
Roger Christian & Co.

Designer
Roger Christian

Alamo Family Foot Care, P.A.

Client
National Center for
Supercomputing Applications,
Education Division

Design Firm
Jack Davis Graphics

NCSA Education Division

Designer
Jack W. Davis

Client
Corning Incorporated

Design Firm
Michael Orr + Associates, Inc.

Designers
Michael R. Orr, Thomas Freeland

CorningOrientation

redley™

Client
Redley

Design Firm
The Traver Company

Designer
Dale Hart

Client
Oveissi Fine Rugs

Design Firm
JLN Design

Designers
Jerril L. Nilson, Terry Duffy

Client
Martin & Glantz

Design Firm
Visible Ink

Designer
Sharon Constant

Client
Tribe

Design Firm
AERIAL

Designers
Tracy Moon, Kimberly Cross

Client
New Destiny Films

Design Firm
Dotzler Creative Arts

LAMSON, DUGAN & MURRAY

Client
Lamson, Dugan & Murray

Design Firm
Dotzler Creative Arts

Client
Resource Renewal

Design Firm
Anvil Graphic Design

Designer
Gary Wong

Client
Centrex, Incorporated

Design Firm
Striegel & Associates

Designers
Peggy Striegel, Dustin Staiger

Client
Violet

Design Firm
AERIAL

Designers
Tracy Moon,
Amanda Troyer,
Stephanie West

Client
impact

Design Firm
AERIAL

Designer
Tracy Moon

Client
Troy Physicians Group

Design Firm
Ford & Earl Associates

Designer
Joseph Becker

HydroDesigns

the precise people

Client
Hydro Designs

Design Firm
Ford & Earl Associates

Designer
Joseph Becker

Client
St. John Health System

Design Firm
Ford & Earl Associates

Designers
Bonnie Detloff Zielinski, Susan Garret

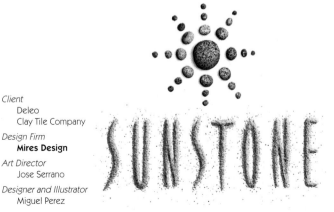

Client
Deleo
Clay Tile Company

Design Firm
Mires Design

Art Director
Jose Serrano

Designer and Illustrator
Miguel Perez

Client
Invitrogen

Design Firm
Mires Design

Art Director
Jose Serrano

Designer and Illustrator
Miguel Perez

274

Client
Ecast

Design Firm
Tsuchiya Sloneker Communications

Creative Director
Julie Tsuchiya

Designer
Andy Harding

A M B R O S I A
taste life

Client
Ambrosia

Design Firm
Tsuchiya Sloneker Communications

Creative Director
Julie Tsuchiya

Art Director
Mark Sloneker

Designer
Colin O'Neill

LEAP™

Client
Leap Energy and Power Corp.

Design Firm
Desgrippes Gobé

Creative Director
Phyllis Aragaki

Senior Designer
Natalie Jacobs

Client
Egad Dzyn

Design Firm
Egad Dzyn

Designer
Steve Trapero

Client
West Hills Hospital & Medical Center

Design Firm
Egad Dzyn

Designer
Steve Trapero

Client
Sólás

Design Firm
Spring Design Group, Inc.

Designers
Stuart Lowitt, Virna Gonzalez

Client
American Tourister

Design Firm
Spring Design Group, Inc.

Designers
Stuart Lowitt, Virna Gonzalez

Client
Integrated Research

Design Firm
Egad Dzyn

Designer
Steve Trapero

275

Client
Interstep

Design Firm
Richland Design Associates

Designers
Doug Fortado, Judith Richland

Attorneys

Client
Sonnenschein, Nath & Rosenthal

Design Firm
Greenfield/Belser Ltd.

Art Director
Burkey Belser

Designer
Jeanette Nuzum

Client
RMF Strategies

Design Firm
Richland Design Associates

Designers
Doug Fortado, Judith Richland

Design Firm
Sign Here, Inc.

Designer
Lori Reynolds

Client
Glazed Expressions

Design Firm
Sayles Graphic Design

Designer
John Sayles

Client
Chap's Creek Welsh Terriers

Design Firm
Art Boy Inc.

Designer
Jane Terzis

Client
Joie de Vivre
Hospitality

Design Firm
**Hunt Weber Clark
Assoc., Inc.**

Designers
Nancy Hunt-Weber,
Christine Chung

everything fabulous

Client
everything fabulous

Design Firm
Anvil Graphic Design

Designer
Faye Roels

archinetix

Architecture for Computing Infrastructures and Networks

Client
archinetix

Design Firm
Jeff Fisher LogoMotives

Designer
Jeff Fisher

Market Perspectives Group Inc.

Client
Market Perspectives Group, Inc.

Design Firm
Shawver Associates

Designer
Amy Krachenfels

Client
East Village
Neighborhood and
Merchants
Association

Design Firm
Sayles Graphic Design

Designer
John Sayles

Client
DaVinci Capital Management

Design Firm
Doerr Associates, Inc.

Designer
Jeannine Baldomero

 **WALKER**
PARKING CONSULTANTS

Client
Walker Parking Consultants

Design Firm
Doerr Associates, Inc.

Designer
Jeannine Baldomero

Client
Active Motif

Design Firm
Laura Coe Design Assoc.

Designer
Ryoichi Yotsumoto

277

Fannie Mae

Client
Rulespace

Design Firm
ID, Incorporated

Designer
Karen Wippich

Client
Fannie Mae

Design Firm
Graves Fowler Associates

Designer
Victoria Q. Robinson

Client
R.F. Stearns

Design Firm
ID, Incorporated

Designer
Shari Chapman

Client
Wright
Veterinary Center

Design Firm
Shubz Graphics

Designer
Jeff Shubzda

Client
Gnibus
Public
Relations

Design Firm
**The
Wecker
Group**

Designer
Matt Gnibus

Client
David Loop European

Design Firm
The Wecker Group

Designer
Robert Wecker,
Matt Gnibus

Client
Haese, LLC

Design Firm
Amisano Design

Designers
Christine Amisano, Dianne Tine

Client
SOLD 4U—Consignment Center

Design Firm
Michael Lee Advertising & Design, Inc.

Designer
Michael Lee

278

Client
Fannie Mae

Design Firm
Graves Fowler Associates

Designer
Esther J. Kang

Client
Adventure Marketing

Design Firm
Buchanan Design

Designers
Bobby Buchanan, Armando Abundis

Carlson West Povondra **Architects**

Client
Carlson West Povondra Architects

Design Firm
Webster Design Associates

Designers
Nate Perry, Dave Webster

Client
Tallgrass Beef

Design Firm
Gardner Design

Designers
Bill Gardner, Brian Miller

Client
Haynes Security Inc.

Design Firm
De Martino Design

Designer
Erik De Martino

Client
Iconixx

Design Firm
Iconixx

Designers
Sid Barcelona, Dave Wiseman

Client
Pontio Communications

Design Firm
Webster Design

Designers
Derek McClure, Dave Webster

Client
World Guaranty

Design Firm
Emmerling Post

Designer
Stuart Cohen

279

Client
Fowler Farms

Design Firm
McElveney & Palozzi Design Group, Inc.

Designers
William McElveney, Matt Nowicki, Jan Marie Gallagher

Client
Oxmoor
Center

Design Firm
**Abney/Huninghake
Design Group**

Designer
Doreen Dehart

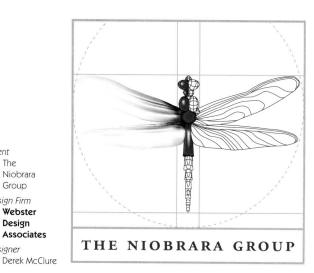

Client
The
Niobrara
Group

Design Firm
**Webster
Design
Associates**

Designer
Derek McClure

Client
PC Assistance Incorporated

Design Firm
McElveney & Palozzi Design Group, Inc.

Designers
William McElveney, Lisa Williamson

Client
Wired
Environments/
DataTone

Design Firm
**Mike Quon/
Designation Inc.**

Designer
Mike Quon

Client
Oracle

Design Firm
Oracle

Art Director
Jeannie Choi

Designer
Leo Kopelow

Client
envestnet

Design Firm
Christopher Gorz Design

Designer
Chris Gorz

Client
Harvest Moon

Design Firm
Adkins/Balchunas

Designers
Jerry Balchunas, Susan DeAngelis

Client
Skills USA—
VICA

Design Firm
Jim Nuttle, Inc.

Designer
Jim Nuttle

Client
pollen 8 studios

Design Firm
pollen 8 studios

Designer
Cory Sheehan

Client
Utilx

Design Firm
Belyea

Designers
Patricia Belyea, Ron Lars Hansen

Client
The
Athenaeum
Fund

Design Firm
Dennis S. Juett
& Associates

Designer
Dennis Scott Juett

Client
DiversityNetwork

Design Firm
Jeff Fisher LogoMotives

Designer
Jeff Fisher

Client
G-Force Collaborations

Design Firm
McElveney & Palozzi Design Group, Inc.

Designers
Matt Nowicki, Dillon Constable, William McElveney

Client
Auto-Soft

Design Firm
McElveney & Palozzi Design Group, Inc.

Designers
Jon Westfall, Steve Palozzi

Client
Shea Homes

Design Firm
Conover

Designers
David Conover, Melissa Fraser

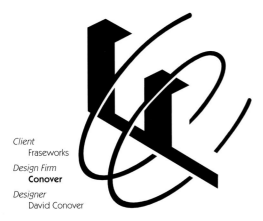

Client
Fraseworks

Design Firm
Conover

Designer
David Conover

Client
Christopher Dental, Ltd.

Design Firm
Creative Dynamics

Designer
Victor Rodriguez

Client
LPA Software

Design Firm
McElveney & Palozzi Design Group, Inc.

Designers
Steve Palozzi, Matt Nowicki, Paul Reisinger, Jr.

Client
Meredith & Crew

Design Firm
Belyea

Designers
Patricia Belyea, Naomi Murphy

Client
Hire Systems

Design Firm
Visigy

Designers
Chris Ardito, Dan Liew, Phorest Bateson

Client
Factura

Design Firm
McElveney & Palozzi Design Group, Inc.

Designers
Steve Palozzi, Matt Nowicki

282

Client
Northchurch
Communications

Design Firm
Jacobs Creative Group

Designer
Priscilla White Sturges

Client
@Risk, Inc.

Design Firm
LF Banks + Associates

Designer
John German

Client
Cee 3 Design

Design Firm
Richard Zeid Design

Designer
Richard Zeid

Center
for Greater Philadelphia

Client
Center for
Greater Philadelphia

Design Firm
LF Banks + Associates

Designers
Lori F. Banks, John German

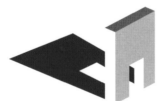

Client
Veenendaal Cave

Design Firm
Belyea

Designers
Patricia Belyea,
Anne Dougherty

Client
KMC Services LLC

Design Firm
Emphasis Seven Communications, Inc.

Designers
Debra L. Nemeth, Todd Land

Client
Addison Homes

Design Firm
Conover

Designers
David Conover,
Amy Williams

TURN OF THE CENTURY STYLE

Client
Mount Mercy Academy

Design Firm
Crowley Webb And Associates

Designer
Dion Pender

283

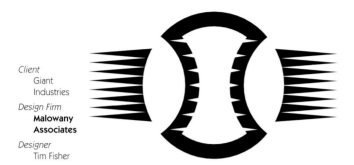

Client
Giant
Industries

Design Firm
**Malowany
Associates**

Designer
Tim Fisher

FOUNDATION
FOR BOULDER VALLEY SCHOOLS

Client
Foundation for
Boulder Valley
Schools

Design Firm
**Malowany
Associates**

Designers
Alan Hesker,
Gene Malowany

Client
Nature Center at Shaker Lakes

Design Firm
**Epstein
Design
Partners Inc.**

Designers
Gina Linehan, Marla Gutzwiller

The Evergreen Society

Client
Digital Realtor

Design Firm
Poonja Design

Designer
Suleman Poonja

Client
Fuse

Design Firm
Fuse

Designer
Russell Pierce

Client
The Greenbrier School

Design Firm
Fuller Designs, Inc.

Designer
Doug Fuller

Client
Monsanto Company/
Nidus Center

Design Firm
**Phoenix
Creative,
St. Louis**

Designer
Ed Mantels-Seeker

Client
Sunriver
Preparatory
School

Design Firm
**Jeff Fisher
LogoMotives**

Creative Director
Sue Fisher

Designer
Jeff Fisher

284

crescent
systems
A software consulting group

Client
Crescent Systems

Design Firm
Tim Kenney Design Partners

Creative Director
Tim Kenney

Designer
Jamie Stockie

Client
Murder City Players

Design Firm
Phoenix Creative, St. Louis

Designer
Ed Mantels-Seeker

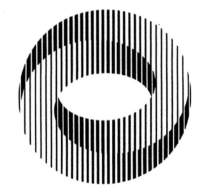

Client
ODC

Design Firm
**Tim Kenney
Design Partners**

Creative Director
Tom Snorek

Designer
Tim Kenney

QUAIL RANCH
A natural way of life

Client
Quail Ranch

Design Firm
Rick Johnson & Company

Designers
Tim McGrath, Lisa Graff

Copywriter
Katie Duberry

Client
Reptile Artists Agent

Design Firm
**Liska +
Associates, Inc.**

Designer
Holle Andersen

Client
Effron

Design Firm
**Handler
Design
Group**

Designer
Bruce Handler

285

Client
Women's
Resource
Center

Design Firm
**Rick Johnson
& Company, Inc.**

Designer
Tim McGrath

Client
Edit Sweet

Design Firm
DHI Visual Communication

Designer
Tuan Do

Come, Experience, and Grow

Client
iBelieve.com

Design Firm
Liska + Associates, Inc.

Designers
Liska + Associates, Inc. Staff

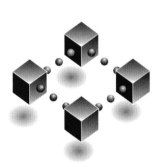

ABITOR

Client
Abitor

Design Firm
**FOCUS
Design
and
Marketing
Solutions**

Creative Director, and Designer
Aram Youssefian

Client
Reliant
Energy

Design Firm
**Lister
Butler
Consulting**

Senior Designer
William Davis

Client
NeuStar, Inc.

Design Firm
Iconixx

Designers
John Cabot Lodge,
Lara Santos

Client
Art O Mat
Design

Design Firm
**Art O Mat
Design**

Designers
Jacki McCarthy,
Mark Kaufman

Art O Mat Design

Client
Excelente Multimedia

Design Firm
Lekas Miller Design

Designer
Lana Ip

Client
Spaceway

Design Firm
FOCUS Design and Marketing Solutions

Designer
Aram Youssefian

Client
Ascent
Leadership
Consortium

Design Firm
**Bullet
Communications, Inc.**

Designer
Tim Scott

Client
Hallin
Construction
Consulting

Design Firm
Conflux Design

Designer
Greg Fedorev

Client
Emergent, Inc.

Design Firm
**DHI
Visual
Communication**

Designer
Dean Sprague

Client
Atwood Mobile Products

Design Firm
Conflux Design

Designer
Greg Fedorev

Client
KidStuff
Public
Relations

Design Firm
**Jeff Fisher
LogoMotives**

Designer
Jeff Fisher

Client
Silution Corporation

Design Firm
**FOCUS
Design and Marketing
Solutions**

Designer
Aram Youssefian

Client
Newpak
USA
Inc.

Design Firm
**Lekas Miller
Design**

Designer
Lana Ip

287

Client
Healthcare
Expense
Reduction
Organization

Design Firm
**Haan & Associates
Advertising Inc.**

Designer
Li Zhang

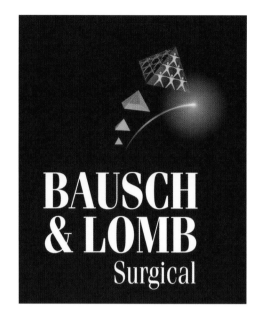

Client
Bausch & Lomb
Surgical

Design Firm
**The
Dupuis
Group**

Designers
Bill Corridori,
Jack Halpern

Rangoon News Bureau

Client
David Carter
Graphic Design
Associates

Design Firm
LoBue Creative

Designer
Gary LoBue, Jr.

Client
Simmons, Ungar, Helbush, Steinberg & Bright

Design Firm
Bruce Yelaska Design

Art Director and Designer
Bruce Yelaska

Client
Rusack Vineyards

Design Firm
Pierre Rademaker Design

Designers
Pierre Rademaker, Jeff Austin

Client
Amarok

Design Firm
**Morgan &
Company**

Designers
Steve Smit,
Andrew Wicklund

288

Client
San Luis Obispo Chamber of Commerce

Design Firm
Pierre Rademaker Design

Designers
Pierre Rademaker, Elisa Ahlin, Kenny Chavez, Debbie Shibata

Client
PairGain

Design Firm
Fuse

Designer
Mike Esparanza

Client
Aria Model & Talent Agency

Design Firm
Liska + Associates, Inc.

Designers
Steve Liska, Kim Fry

Client
Little Angels

Design Firm
KKD

Designer
Karl Kromer

Client
Championship Publishing, LLC

Design Firm
Goodson + Yu Design Ltd.

Designer
Roger Yu

Client
Pensare

Design Firm
Visigy

Designers
Linda Kelley, Suzy Leung

Client
Xerox

Design Firm
Wunderman Cato Johnson/San Francisco

Executive Creative Director
John Meyer

Art Director
Sylvia Grossman

Client
Pfizer Inc.

Design Firm
Hans Flink Design Inc.

Designer
Chang-Mei Lin

289

Client
Unilever HPC, USA
Design Firm
Hans Flink Design Inc.
Designers
Michael Troian, Harry Bertschmann

Client
Colgate-Palmolive
Design Firm
Hans Flink Design Inc.
Designers
Mark Krukonis, Susan Kunschaft

Client
Brainplay.com
Design Firm
Leopard
Designers
Brendan Hemp, Nita Herupermatasari

Client
Cirqit.com
Design Firm
Leopard
Designer
Nita Herupermatasari

Client
Lighthouse Holdings
Design Firm
Kendra Power Design & Communication
Designer
Larkin Werner

Client
Intellisol International
Design Firm
Hedstrom/Blessing Inc.
Designer
Mike Goebel

Client
Jwana Juice
Design Firm
Cathey Associates, Inc.
Designer
Isabel Campos

Client
The Pittsburgh Symphony
Design Firm
Kendra Power Design & Communication
Designer
Kathy Kendra

290

Client
Hello Central

Design Firm
Pierre Rademaker Design

Designers
Pierre Rademaker, Jeff Austin

ELECTRONIC PAYMENTS NETWORK
AUTOMATED CLEARING HOUSE SERVICES

Client
Electronic
Payments
Network

Design Firm
**Rowe
Design Group**

Designer
Edward L. Rowe, Jr.

Client
Tippacanoe
County
Public Library

Design Firm
**Indiana
Design
Consortium, Inc.**

Designer
Patrick Nycz

TIPPECANOE COUNTY
PUBLIC LIBRARY

Client
Pairgain

Design Firm
FUSE

Designer
Russell Pierce

Client
G. Lazzara Logo
(Writing and
Public Relations
Planning)

Design Firm
Icon Graphics, Inc.

Designer
Icon Graphics, Inc.

**DENNY
EYE & LASER
CENTER**

Client
Denny Eye & Laser Center

Design Firm
Hunt Weber Clark Assoc., Inc.

Designers
Christine Chung, Nancy Hunt-Weber

Client
Hawthorne Lane

Design Firm
**Hunt Weber Clark
Assoc., Inc.**

Designers
Nancy Hunt-Weber,
Jason Bell

Client
@pos.com

Design Firm
Michael Patrick Partners

Design Director
Darice Koziel

Designers
Connie Hwang, Victoria Pohlmann

E✳TRADE®

Client
S1 Corporation

Design Firm
Michael Patrick Partners

Design Director
Darice Koziel

Designers
Connie Hwang, Ian Smith

Client
E*Trade

Design Firm
Michael Patrick Partners

Design Director
Dan O'Brien

Designers
Matt Sanders, Connie Hwang

ICarian

aspirian

Client
Icarian

Design Firm
Michael Patrick Partners

Design Director
Mike Mescall

Designers
Ian Smith, Sam Chew

Client
Aspirian

Design Firm
Michael Patrick Partners

Design Director
Dan O'Brien

Designers
Matt Sanders, Connie Hwang

electricwindow

Client
ElectricWindow.com

Design Firm
Michael Patrick Partners

Design Director
Katie Bush

Designers
Eko Tjoek, Matt Rowland

Kodak
SCREENCHECK
EXPERIENCE

Client
Eastman Kodak

Design Firm
**Tsuchiya Sloneker
Communications**

Designers
Julie Tsuchiya,
Colin O'Neill

292

Client
Hitachi Data Systems

Design Firm
Hitachi Data Systems
Marketing Communications

Designer
Michael McCann

iLAB

Client
Hitachi Data Systems

Design Firm
Hitachi Data Systems
Marketing Communications

Designer
Barry Chan

RESOURCE

Client
Resource 1 Construction Services

Design Firm
Five Visual Communication & Design

Designers
Denny Fagan, Rondi Tschopp

A   R   M   T

Client
Assisted
Reproductive
Medical
Technologies

Design Firm
John Kneapler
Design

Designers
Holly Buckley,
John Kneapler

Smart**Ship**.com

Client
Smartship.com

Design Firm
Evenson Design Group

Designer
Karen Barranco

D O U B L E G R E E N
L A N D S C A P E S

Client
Double Green

Design Firm
Evenson Design Group

Designer
Judy Lee

Winfire™

Client
Winfire

Design Firm
Evenson Design Group

Designers
Karen Barranco, Mark Sojka

   atrieva

Client
Atrieva

Design Firm
Michael Patrick
Partners

Design Director
Katie Bush

Designers
Matt Rowland,
Eko Tjoek

Client
National Kidney Foundation

Design Firm
KBB Communications Design

Designer
Shelby Carcio

Client
Icon
Restoration

Design Firm
**B-Man
Design**

Designer
Eric Etheridge

NIMH

Client
National Institute of Mental Health

Design Firm
HC Creative Communications

Designer
David Hazelton

Client
World Wide
Sports

Design Firm
**Compass
Design**

Designers
Mitchell
Lindgren,
Tom Arthur,
Rich McGowen

Client
Triumph Title

Design Firm
Ford & Earl Associates

Designer
Francheska Guerrero

Client
Stone Horse

Design Firm
Walsh Associates

Designer
Mike Donahue

CEDAR MOUNTAIN SCIENCE CENTER

DEVOTED TO ENVIRONMENTAL EDUCATION ·
LIVING AND INTERACTING WHERE ONE LIVES

Client
Cedar Mountain
Science Center

Design Firm
Weller Institute

Designer
Don Weller

Client
Acadio Corporation

Design Firm
Werkhaus Creative Communications

Designers
Thad Boss, James Sundstad

294

Leadership**Impact**

Client
Leadership Impact

Design Firm
Michael Orr + Associates, Inc.

Designer
Michael R. Orr

Client
World Wide
Sports

Design Firm
Compass Design

Designers
Mitchell Lindgren,
Tom Arthur,
Rich McGowen

SUNRISE GOURMET™

Client
Sunrise Gourmet

Design Firm
Compass Design

Designers
Mitchell Lindgren, Tom Arthur, Rich McGowen

NE**X**TLINX™

Client
NextLinx Corporation

Design Firm
HC Creative Communications

Designer
Ann Marie Ternullo

Client
World Wide
Sports

Design Firm
Compass Design

Designers
Mitchell Lindgren,
Tom Arthur,
Rich McGowen

**The Citizens
National Bank**
of Southwestern Ohio

Client
The Citizens National Bank

Design Firm
Design Forum

Designer
Vivienne Padilla

295

Client
YWCA

Design Firm
Hershey Associates

Designers
R. Christine Hershey, Lisa Joss

Client
Anton Airfoods

Design Firm
Design Forum

Designers
Vivienne B. Padilla

RiverRidge
a planned community in a woodland setting

Client
Miami University

Design Firm
Peg Faimon Design

Designer
Peg Faimon

Client
Kasprzak Condominiums, Inc.

Design Firm
Jasper & Bridge

Designers
Alexander Bridge, Kim Noyes

Client
Leggat McCall Properties

Design Firm
Doerr Associates, Inc.

Designer
Lauren Jeuick

Client
Susan Love

Design Firm
Hershey Associates

Designers
R. Christine Hershey, Lisa Joss

Client
Riverbed
Technologies

Design Firm
**EVD
Advertising**

Designers
Rachel Deutsch,
Marc Foelsch

Client
Pet Talk!

Design Firm
Handler Design Group

Designer
Bruce Handler

296

Client
Powerize

Design Firm
EVD Advertising

Designers
Rachel Deutsch, Tom Cosgrove

Client
Harvest
Consulting
Group, LLC

Design Firm
**Cullinane
Design**

Designer
Charl Kroeger

Client
Hotel Metropole—Catalina Island

Design Firm
Dalton Design Inc.

Designer
Annmarie Dalton

Client
Enterworks

Design Firm
EVD Advertising

Designers
Rachel Deutsch, Blake Stenning, Marc Foelsch

Client
Taco Bueno

Design Firm
Pentagram

Designer
Lowell Williams

Client
Dalton
Design
Inc.

Design Firm
**Dalton
Design
Inc.**

Designer
Annmarie Dalton

Client
WISEPlace

Design Firm
**Engle
+
Murphy**

Designer
Emily Moe

Client
Blake Printery

Design Firm
**Pierre Rademaker
Design**

Designers
Pierre Rademaker,
Randy David

efiltration

Client
Filtration
Group

Design Firm
Identity Center

Designers
Wayne Kosterman, Matt Nelson

Client
Vacation Ownership

Design Firm
**Schwener
Design Group**

Designers
Diane Schwener,
Frank Martin

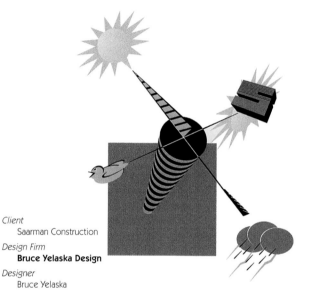

Client
Saarman Construction

Design Firm
Bruce Yelaska Design

Designer
Bruce Yelaska

Client
Motorola
Semiconductor
Components
Group

Design Firm
Pentagram

Designer
Wendy Carnegie

ADULTCARE
Centers of America

COASTALVIEW
AdultCare Center

Client
AdultCare Centers of America

Design Firm
Jasper & Bridge

Designers
Alexander Bridge, Kim Noyes

VILLAGEMANOR
AdultCare Center

PARKVIEW
AdultCare Center

Fox Festival 2000

Client
foxdream.com

Design Firm
Imtech Communications

Designer
Robert Keng

shipper.com

Client
Shipper.com

Design Firm
Bright Strategic Design

Designers
Keith Bright, Denis Parkhurst

Client
A Mixed Bag

Design Firm
Ogburn Design

Designer
Sharon R. Ogburn

Client
A Taste of Arlington

Design Firm
EVD Advertising

Designers
Rachel Deutsch,
Marc Foelsch

LA2012

Client
Los Angeles
Olympic Committee

Design Firm
Bright Strategic Design

Designer
Keith Bright

Client
Purdue University

Design Firm
Purdue University

Designer
Li Zhang

Client
NetZero, Inc.

Design Firm
Bright Strategic Design

Designer
Keith Bright

Client
Mandalay Pictures

Design Firm
Bright Strategic Design

Designers
Keith Bright, Ray Wood

Client
Back At Ya Web Design

Design Firm
Wet Paper Bag Graphic Design

Designer
Lewis Glaser

Client
Innovative Mortgage Solutions

Design Firm
Imtech Communications

Designer
Robert Keng

Client
AT&T Corporation

Design Firm
Bright Strategic Design

Designers
Keith Bright, Chad White

Client
ResourceLink

Design Firm
Glyphix Studio

Designer
Eric Sena

OUTDOOR SERVICES

Client
Outdoor Services

Design Firm
Glyphix Studio

Designer
Brad Wilder

Client
Joe To-Go

Design Firm
KKD

Designers
Karl Kromer, Kim Mattos

300

Client
Interactive
Market
System

Design Firm
EHR Design

Designers
Mark Rue,
Daniel Sandbach

Client
Xyvision
Enterprise
Solutions, Inc.

Design Firm
**Stewart Monderer
Design, Inc.**

Designer
Stewart Monderer

Client
redbricks.com

Client
US Felt

Design Firm
Jasper & Bridge

Designers
Alexander Bridge,
Andy Thorington

Client
BroadStream

Design Firm
Glyphix Studio

Designer
Brad Wilder

Client
FilterTech

Design Firm
EHR Design

Designers
Brian Eickhoff, Ashley Edwards

Client
Kallix Corporation

Design Firm
**Stewart Monderer
Design, Inc.**

Designer
Stewart Monderer

Client
Medschool.com

Design Firm
Bright Strategic Design

Designers
Keith Bright, Stephanie Tsao

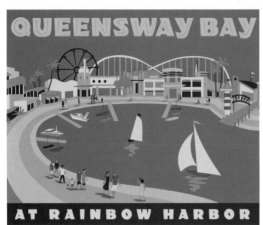

Client
Oliver McMillan

Design Firm
Sabingrafik, Inc.

Designer
Tracy Sabin

Client
IMLOGO

Design Firm
Imtech Communications

Designer
Robert Keng

Client
Chinatown YMCA

Design Firm
Imtech Communications

Designer
Robert Keng

Client
Oliver McMillan

Design Firm
Sabingrafik, Inc.

Designer
Tracy Sabin

Client
Sirgany
Sunset, LLC

Design Firm
**Pavlik
Design Team**

Designer
Renée Farrugia

Client
Jade Solutions

Design Firm
Communication Arts, Inc.

Art Director
Richard Foy

Designer
Dave Dute

302

centricity

Client
  Centricity
Design Firm
  FUSE
Designer
  Russell Pierce

ELM RIDGE

Client
  Elm Ridge
Design Firm
  inc 3
Designers
  Harvey Applebaum,
  Ayse Celem

sounds

Client
  Casade Musica de Luxe
Design Firm
  Pavlik Design Team
Designer
  Renée Farrugia

SHAMAN
Good Medicine For Technology

Client
  Shaman
Design Firm
  Diesel Design
Designer
  Amy Bainbridge

Client
  University
  of Nevada
  Las Vegas
Design Firm
  **Rick Johnson
  & Company, Inc.**
Designer
  Tim McGrath

Ceiva

Client
  Idea Grove
Design Firm
  Bright Strategic Design
Designers
  Keith Bright, Weina Dinata, Richard Vasquez

Client
  El Cholo
  Cantina
Design Firm
  **Maddocks
  & Co.**
Designers
  Clare Sebenius,
  Tracy Sabin

QORUS.COM

Client
  Qorus.com
Design Firm
  Bright Strategic Design
Designers
  Keith Bright, Denis Parkhurst

gREPTILE GRIP ™

FATHOMS

EASTLAKE
TRAILS

**Systemic
Solutions**
Incorporated

PEARL MOON
BOUTIQUE

crescent
consulting

www.goinet.com

CLASSIC Ⓒ MEDIA

Client
KMC Telecom Inc.

Design Firm
Emphasis Seven Communications, Inc.

Designer
Debra L. Nemeth

Client
Dal Lido Restaurant

Design Firm
Bullet Communications, Inc.

Designer
Tim Scott

Client
Abacus Restaurant, Dallas, Texas

Design Firm
David Carter Graphic Design

Creative Director
Lori Wilson

Designer
Emily Cain

A B A C U S

O C E A N P L A C E

Client
Oliver McMillan

Design Firm
Sabingrafik, Inc.

Designer
Tracy Sabin

kn⬤wledgenet

Client
KnowledgeNet

Design Firm
Kendra Power Design & Communication

Designer
Larkin Werner

Client
The Mansion
at MGM Grand,
Las Vegas, Nevada

Design Firm
**David Carter
Graphic Design**

Creative Director
Lori Wilson

Designer
Ashley Barron

THE MANSION
at MGM Grand

GRANE
HEALTHCARE

Client
Grane Healthcare

Design Firm
A to Z communications, inc.

Designer
Richard Hooper

MISSION

Client
The Richard E. Jacobs Group

Design Firm
Herip Associates

Designers
Walter Herip,
John Menter

305

Gaslamp
SIXTH AVENUE

Client
Oliver McMillan

Design Firm
Sabingrafik, Inc.

Designer
Tracy Sabin

Client
City of Boulder

Design Firm
Communication Arts, Inc.

Art Director
Dave Tweed

Designer
Traci Jones

Client
Portifino Bay Hotel, Ordando, Florida

Design Firm
David Carter Graphic Design

Creative Director   *Designer*
Lori Wilson   Emily Cain

BROUILLETTE
GREATER METRO

Client
Brouillette Greater Metro

Design Firm
Liz J. Design, Inc.

Designer
Nancy Hauck

Client
Atlantis
Resort and Casino,
Nassau, The Bahamas

Design Firm
**David Carter
Graphic Design**

Creative Director
Lori Wilson

Designer
Tien Pham

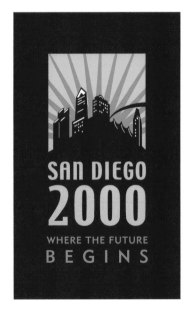

Client
San Diego Convis

Design Firm
Dizinno and Partners

Designers
Mike Stivers,
Tracy Sabin

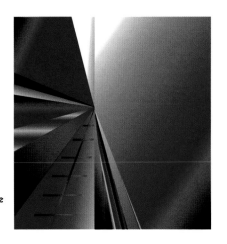

Client
Michael Charek
Architects

Design Firm
Jasper & Bridge

Designer
Kim Noyes

Client
Hunan Garden

Design Firm
Bruce Yelaska Design

Designers
Bruce Yelaska

Client
Madalay Bay
Resort and Casino,
Las Vegas, Nevada

Design Firm
**David Carter
Graphic Design**

Creative Director
Lori Wilson

Designer
Sharon LeJeune

SHANGHAI
L I L L Y

Client
youticket.com

Design Firm
**Tusk
Studios**

Designers
Virginia Thompson,
Paul Rippens

LoansDirect℠

Client
LoansDirect

Design Firm
Engle + Murphy

Designer
Chancie Gannin

Client
City of Boulder

Design Firm
Communication Arts, Inc.

Art Director
Richard Foy

Designer
Dave Tweed

GeoTrust℠

Client
GeoTrust

Design Firm
Belyea

Designers
Patricia Belyea,
Ron Lars Hansen

Client
The Mills Corporation

Design Firm
Communication Arts, Inc.

Art Director
Henry Beer

Designer
Traci Jones

307

I N H S

INLAND NORTHWEST HEALTH SERVICES

Client
Inland Northwest Health Services

Design Firm
Klundt Hosmer Design

Designers
Darin Klundt, Henry Ortega

Client
Rue 21

Design Firm
JGA, Inc.

Designers
Brian Eastman,
Tony Camilletti

Client
Skills USA VICA

Design Firm
Jim Nuttle, Inc.

Designer
Jim Nuttle

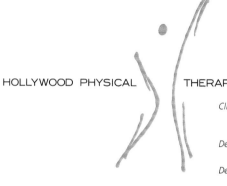

HOLLYWOOD PHYSICAL THERAPY ASSOCIATES

Client
Hollywood
Physical Therapy Associates

Design Firm
Asylum

Designers
Jim Shanman,
Andrea Wynnyk

Client
Auto-Soft

Design Firm
McElveney & Palozzi Design Group, Inc.

Designers
Jon Westfall, Steve Palozzi

Client
Flexographic Technical Association

Design Firm
Callery & Company

Designer
Kelley Callery

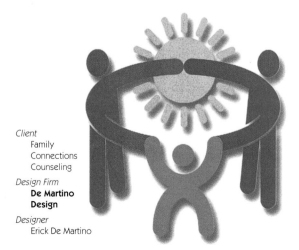

Client
Family
Connections
Counseling

Design Firm
**De Martino
Design**

Designer
Erick De Martino

Client
Mirapoint, Inc.

Design Firm
Mortensen Design

Art Director
Gordon Mortensen

Designer
PJ Nidecker

ATLANTIS
R E S T A U R A N T

Client
Atlantis Restaurant

Design Firm
pollen 8 studios

Designer
Cory Sheehan

FirstChip

Client
Micheal Waits

Design Firm
Koch Creative Services

Designer
Brod Ruder

Client
Whitehall Capital & Assoc.

Design Firm
De Martino Design

Designer
Erick De Martino

Client
Hamilton Ink

Design Firm
De Martino Design

Designer
Erick De Martino

Client
Go Biz Go

Design Firm
Cahan & Associate

Art Director
Bill Cahan

Designer
Craig Bailey

Client
Apex Signs & Graphics

Design Firm
Full Steam Marketing & Design

Designer
Lori Hughes

Presbytery of Philadelphia

Client
Presbytery of Philadelphia

Design Firm
Art 270, Inc.

Designers
Sean Flanagan, Holly Kempf, Carl Mill

Client
Bald Beaver
Brewing Co.

Design Firm
**David Lemley
Design**

Designers
David Lemley,
Emma Wilson

Client
Tippecanoe
County
Public
Library

Design Firm
Pandora

Designer
Silvia Grossmann

TIPPECANOE COUNTY PUBLIC LIBRARY

INTERVENTIONS FOR BEHAVIORAL CHANGE

Client
Interventions for Behavioral Change

Design Firm
Steve Morris

Designer
Steve Morris

Multimedia
Telesys, Inc.

Client
Multimedia Telesys, Inc.

Design Firm
Sanft Design Inc.

Designers
Alfred C. Sanft,
Paul Howell

Client
Narada

Design Firm
Cahan & Associates

Art Director
Bill Cahan

Designer
Sharrie Brooks

N A R A D A ®

Client
Terranova

Design Firm
**Full Steam
Marketing & Design**

Designer
Peter Hester

310

Client
nextHR

Design Firm
**Wages
Design**

Designer
Matt Taylor

CineMaster™

Client
Ravisent
Technologies

Design Firm
Art 270, Inc.

Designer
Sean Flanagan

RAD IUS
product development

Client
Radius
Product Development

Design Firm
Arc Design

Designers
Jac Phillips, Kevin O'Leary, Kevin Bergen, Todd Kinniburgh

Client
Stoked Media

Design Firm
Full Steam Marketing & Design

Designers
Bill Owen, Peter Hester

POWER
TRAVEL

Client
Power Travel

Design Firm
Guarino Graphics & Design Studio

Designer
Jan Guarino

iProTalk

Client
iProTalk

Design Firm
Cahan & Associates

Art Director
Bill Cahan

Designer
Michael Braley

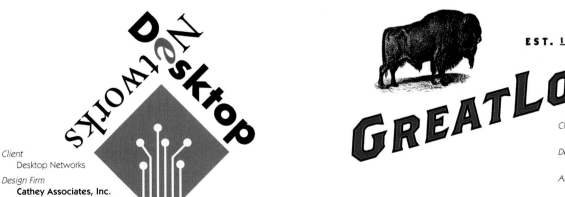

Client
Desktop Networks

Design Firm
Cathey Associates, Inc.

Designers
Matt Westapher, Isabel Campos

EST. 1999

GREATLODGE

Client
Great Lodge

Design Firm
Cahan & Associates

Art Director
Bill Cahan

Designers
Neal Ashby, Sharrie Brooks

311

OnLine **Interpreters**
The Global Connection

Client
Online Interpreters

Design Firm
The Wecker Group

Designer
Robert Wecker

I L S

Client
Adcom

Design Firm
Workhorse Design, Inc.

Designers
Constance Kovar, Anthony Taibi

Client
David Carter
Graphic Design
Associates

Design Firm
LoBue Creative

Designer
Gary LoBue, Jr.

coral reef boutique

Quality Products. Exceptional Response.

Client
FMC Corporations and Solutia

Design Firm
Stan Gellman Graphic Design, Inc.

Designers
Mike Donovan, Barry Tilson

Client
Professional Communicators of Western New York,
Art Directors/Communicators of Buffalo

Design Firm
Crowley Webb And Associates

Designers
David Buck, Karen Sopic, Rob Wynne

Client
Telos Group

Design Firm
Crowley Webb And Associates

Designer
Dion Pender

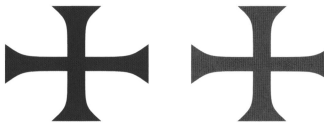

Client
Church of the Beloved

Design Firm
Steve Thomas Marketing Communications

Designer
Steve Thomas

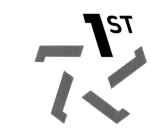

 **FirstBank**

Client
First Bank
of
Burkburnett

Design Firm
Design Works

Designer
Stephen St. John

coca-cola

CAMPUS MARKETING MANAGER

Client
Coca-Cola

Design Firm
Cottril Design

Designer
Allison Cottril

ALTEK

INNOVATIVE

MANUFACTURING

SOLUTIONS

Client
Altek
Manufacturing

Design Firm
**Klundt
Hosmer
Design**

Designers
Darin Klundt,
Tracey Carlson

NINETEEN-NINETY-NINE
BUG OFF
FOLEY SACKETT
SUMMER PICNIC

Client
Foley Sackett

Design Firm
Foley Sackett

Designer
Michelle Willinganz

Client
Downtown
Seattle
Association

Design Firm
**Art O Mat
Design**

Designers
Jacki McCarthy,
Mark Kaufman

Client
Saucy Ree's
Gourmet Foods

Design Firm
**The
Wecker
Group**

Designer
Robert Wecker

NewBandHorizons

Client
American Composers Forum

Design Firm
Foley Sackett

Designer
Tim Moran

Night)Guard

Client
Dental Concepts

Design Firm
Handler Design Group

Designer
Bruce Handler

Continental Harmony

NEW MUSIC FOR THE MILLENNIUM

Client
American
Composers
Forum

Design Firm
Foley Sackett

Designer
Tim Moran

Client
Baykeepers

Design Firm
Cahan & Associates

Art Director
Bill Cahan

Designer
Michael Braley

Sk!p

Client
City of Boulder

Design Firm
Communication Arts, Inc.

Art Director
Dave Tweed

Designer
Karl Hirshman

Client
Galaxy
Online, Inc./
Doug Conway

Design Firm
**B.D. Fox
&
Friends, Inc.
Advertising**

Designer
John Soltis

GALAXYONLINE

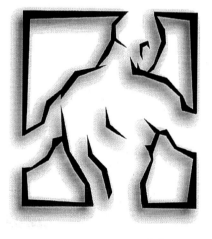

Client
Pain
Rehabilitation
Center

Design Firm
DesignWorks

Designer
Stephen Fleming

Client
Dearfield Tours, LLC

Design Firm
LoBue Creative

Designer
Gary LoBue, Jr.

AEGEAN TOUR LINES

Client
Green Bay
Boy Choir
&
Girl Choir, Inc.

Design Firm
**Daniel Green
Eye-D Design**

Designer
Daniel Green

C O L O R F X

Client
Color FX

Design Firm
Mauck + Associates

Designers
Scott Thornton, Kent Mauck

GeoCities

Client
GeoCities

Design Firm
Landor Associates

Designer
Robert Matza

Client
Full Steam
Marketing
&
Design

Design Firm
**Full Steam
Marketing
&
Design**

Designer
Leslie Sherwin

KING RANCH VINEYARDS

Client
Corporate Concepts

Design Firm
LoBue Creative

Designer
Gary LoBue, Jr.

n-telec media services

Client
Corporate Concepts

Design Firm
LoBue Creative

Designer
Gary LoBue, Jr.

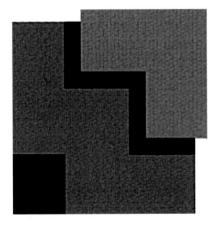

Client
PointConnect

Design Firm
Triad, Inc.

Designer
Michael Dambrowsky

Client
Feel
Good
Records

Design Firm
**Full Steam
Marketing & Design**

Designer
Peter Hester

Client
Gifts.com

Design Firm
Landor Associates

Designers
Pippa White-Golden, Alice Coxe

INDEX

316

318